IN THE NAME
OF ALLAH

HOW ISIS DRENCHED FAITH IN BLOOD

ANDREAS SCHNADERBECK

IMPRINT

Bibliographic information of the German National Library: The German National Library lists this publication in the German National Bibliography; detailed bibliographic data can be accessed on the Internet via http://dnb.dnb.de.

Publisher: BoD · Books on Demand GmbH, In de Tarpen 42, 22848 Norderstedt

Printing: Libri Plureos GmbH, Friedensallee 273, 22763 Hamburg

ISBN: 978-3-7693-0317-9

TABLE OF CONTENTS

FOREWORD

In a world marked by wars and conflicts, the Islamic State (IS) has left a trail of violence and destruction that has deeply shaken humanity. But while his gruesome deeds have dominated the news, it's important to remember that this seemingly overpowering enemy is failing. His ideology, his brutality and his attempts to put the world in fear are nothing more than the last stand of a lost group that will not last in the face of progress, humanity and the unstoppable power of solidarity.

When we talk about ISIS, it seems easy to fall into fear and hopelessness. But a look at reality shows us that this horror must be seen in a larger context. Year after year, more people die from dog attacks, lightning strikes or even the tiny bites of mosquitoes than from ISIS attacks. These comparatively everyday dangers illustrate how small the real threat from ISIS is when compared to the immeasurable strength and resilience of humanity.

ISIS may have tried to plunge the world into darkness, but it underestimated us. Every act of violence has not only had the opposite effect but has also strengthened the will of the people to fight for freedom, peace and humanity. The stories of survivors, of resistance fighters, and of all those who fight tirelessly against the tyranny of ISIS are proof that no regime, no matter how cruel, can ever stand up to humanity's unstoppable drive for freedom.

History shows us that any attempt to oppress humanity ultimately fails. IS is no exception. Just as lightning breaks through only a moment of darkness before the sky becomes light again, so too will ISIS fade in the light of justice and humanity. Let us together find the courage to set out in a world that cannot be brought to its knees by IS. Instead, we walk with our heads held high into a future that is not characterized by terror and fear, but by hope and human cohesion.

EMERGENCE OF THE ISLAMIC STATE

The emergence of the Islamic State (IS) is a multi-layered and historically deep-rooted phenomenon that has developed over several decades. To understand in detail, the emergence of ISIS, it is necessary to examine the ideological foundations, historical developments, and specific political, social, and economic conditions in the region that enabled the emergence of this extremist organization. This comprehensive analysis goes into the various aspects that led to the emergence of ISIS step by step.

The ideological foundations of the Islamic State are deeply rooted in Salafism, a current within Sunni Islam that aims to return to the practices and teachings of the "pious ancestors" (Salaf). Salafism rejects any form of innovation (bid'a) and calls for a strict application of Sharia, Islamic law. This puritanical interpretation of Islam has gained influence over the course of the 20th century, particularly through the promotion of Wahhabism, the official state religion of Saudi Arabia. Wahhabism, named after the scholar Muhammad ibn Abd al-Wahhab, originated in the Arabian Peninsula in the 18th century and propagated a particularly strict and unadulterated form of Islam. This ideology, which was actively supported and exported by the Saudi government, had a major impact on the Islamist movement worldwide, including those who later founded ISIS.

Another central ideological building block of IS is jihadism. This movement interprets jihad, originally a comprehensive term for the "struggle in the way of God", primarily as an armed struggle against the "enemies of Islam". Modern jihadism has its roots in the Egyptian Muslim Brotherhood and has been significantly shaped by the writings of Sayyid Qutb, one of the movement's leading ideologues. Qutb's works, especially "Ma'alim fi al-Tariq" ("Signposts"), called for the fight against the regimes in the Muslim world that were considered "un-Islamic" and for the establishment of an Islamic state. These ideas were later taken up by more radical groups such as al-Qaeda and developed further in a global perspective that legitimized the fight against the "West" and the "un-Islamic" governments in the Islamic world.

The Soviet-Afghan war (1979-1989) played a central role in the development of global jihadism, which later also influenced ISIS. The war attracted thousands of Islamist volunteers from across the Muslim world, who became known as "Afghan Arabs." These fighters joined the Mujahideen, who were supported by the US, Pakistan, Saudi Arabia and other countries, to fight against the Soviet troops and the communist government they supported in Afghanistan. Participation in this war not only strengthened the military potential of these fighters, but also promoted the formation of a transnational network of radicalized Islamists.

This war gave rise to al-Qaeda, an organization founded in 1988 by Osama bin Laden and other radical Islamists. Al-

Qaeda represented a significant development of jihadist ideas, as it regarded the armed struggle against the West and its allies as a priority task. Osama bin Laden and Ayman al-Zawahiri, the leaders of al-Qaeda, saw the "distant enemy" (the West) as the main target, while local jihadist groups often fought the "near enemy" (un-Islamic governments in the Muslim world). The ideology of al-Qaeda and its operational networks formed the ideological and organizational framework from which the Islamic State later emerged.

The invasion of Iraq in 2003 by a US-led coalition had profound and far-reaching consequences for the entire region. The fall of Iraqi dictator Saddam Hussein led to a massive power vacuum that plunged the country into chaos. Two particularly momentous decisions by the US occupation authority were the dissolution of the Iraqi army and the banning of the Baath Party, the ruling party under Saddam Hussein. As a result of these measures, hundreds of thousands of Sunni Iraqis who had worked in state functions and in the army under the Baath regime suddenly found themselves without work and prospects. This disempowerment and marginalization of the Sunni elite in Iraq created a deep bitterness and a sense of injustice that was the breeding ground for the rise of radical groups such as al-Qaeda in Iraq (AQI).

In the chaos that followed the invasion, al-Qaeda in Iraq (AQI) was formed under the leadership of Abu Musab al-Zarqawi, a Jordanian Islamist who had already fought against the Soviets in Afghanistan. Zarqawi was a particularly brutal and ruthless leader whose ideology was marked by extreme violence against Shiites and Western targets. AQI carried out numerous attacks against the Shiite population and US-led troops in Iraq, with the aim of escalating the Sunni-Shiite conflict and plunging the country into a sectarian civil war. While Zarqawi's strategy of maximum violence led to tensions with the leadership of al-Qaeda, which favored a less sectarian approach, it proved effective in further destabilizing Iraq. The Iraq war eventually led to an open civil war between Sunni and Shiite militias, which plunged the country further into chaos. AQI cleverly exploited this conflict to expand its power base and began to control areas in western Iraq. Zarqawi was killed in a US airstrike in 2006, but his group survived and regrouped. In the same year, AQI joined forces with other Sunni rebel groups and founded the "Islamic State in Iraq" (ISI), which is considered the predecessor of the later IS.

The Syrian civil war, which erupted in 2011 as part of the so-called "Arab Spring," provided an opportunity for the ISI to regroup and expand its activities beyond Iraq's borders. The war led to a fragmentation of Syrian society and significantly weakened the central government. Various rebel groups fought for control of the country, and in this chaotic environment, the ISI, now renamed the Islamic State of Iraq and Syria (ISIS), began to seize strategically important areas in eastern Syria. These regions, especially around the city of Raqqa, became important bases of operations for the group.

IS benefited from the power vacuum created by the Syrian civil war. While the Syrian government under Bashar al-Assad was fighting for its survival and international actors were divided over the support of the various rebel groups, IS was able to expand unhindered. The organization relied on a mixture of military force and the establishment of administrative structures to consolidate control over the conquered territories. The revenues from the oil trade, extortion and looting, as well as the recruitment of fighters from abroad, allowed IS to further expand its power base and consolidate its rule.

The culmination of ISIS's expansion was the capture of the northern Iraqi city of Mosul in June 2014. This military success, achieved largely without resistance from the Iraqi army, marked a turning point in the group's history. Mosul, Iraq's second-largest city, was of great strategic importance, both economically and symbolically. By capturing the city, ISIS managed to capture enormous amounts of weapons and funds, which enabled the group to further expand its power.

On June 29, 2014, a few weeks after the conquest of Mosul, Abu Bakr al-Baghdadi proclaimed the "caliphate" and declared himself caliph, the religious and political leader of all Muslims. This proclamation had enormous symbolic significance, as it underlined ISIS's claim to take over the leadership of the global Muslim community and establish an Islamic world empire. The caliphate was portrayed by ISIS as a legitimate successor to the original Islamic caliphate from the time of the Prophet Muhammad, which gave the group both religious legitimacy and a clear ideological identity.

The emergence of the Islamic State was the result of a variety of factors that worked for decades. Ideological currents such as Salafism and jihadism formed the intellectual foundations, while geopolitical events such as the Soviet-Afghan war and the invasion of Iraq by the USA created the military and organizational conditions. The Syrian civil war finally provided the necessary chaos in which IS could establish its power base. The proclamation of the caliphate in 2014 was the culmination of these developments, consolidating ISIS's self-image as a supranational, religious-political authority. At the same time, the emergence of IS shows the devastating effects of regional destabilization, political failure and the uncontrolled spread of radical ideologies. These factors contributed decisively to the emergence of an organization like the Islamic State and for a time to control large parts of Iraq and Syria.

March 2003: The US and its allies begin the invasion of Iraq to overthrow the regime of Saddam Hussein. This leads to a power vacuum and the rise of various rebel groups.

October 2004: Abu Musab al-Zarqawi founds the group "Al-Qaeda in Iraq" (AQI), which later serves as the nucleus for the Islamic State (IS). This group carries out numerous attacks against US troops and Shiite civilians.

January 2006: AQI merges with several other Sunni rebel groups to form the Mujahideen Shura Council.
October 2006: After the death of al-Zarqawi, the group announces the establishment of the "Islamic State in Iraq" (ISI) under the leadership of Abu Omar al-Baghdadi.

April 2010: Abu Bakr al-Baghdadi takes over the leadership of the ISI after the death of Abu Omar al-Baghdadi and the then military commander.

March 2011: The civil war in Syria begins. The ISI is taking advantage of the chaos and expanding its operations into Syria. This leads to the formation of "Jabhat al-Nusra", an offshoot of ISI in Syria.

April 2013: Al-Baghdadi declares the merger of ISI and Jabhat al-Nusra and announces the establishment of the "Islamic State in Iraq and Syria" (ISIS). However, this is rejected by Jabhat al-Nusra, leading to a rift between the two groups.

June 2014: ISIS captures the Iraqi city of Mosul and declares the establishment of a "caliphate" under the leadership of Abu Bakr al-Baghdadi. The Islamic State (IS) is becoming internationally known and attracts numerous foreign fighters.
August 2014: ISIS captures the Yazidi city of Sinjar in northern Iraq and commits serious human rights violations, including massacres and enslavement. The US then begins air strikes against IS positions in Iraq, marking the beginning of a broad international coalition to fight ISIS.

2014-2015: ISIS conquers large areas in Syria and Iraq, including the cities of Raqqa (Syria) and Ramadi (Iraq). Raqqa becomes the de facto capital of the IS caliphate. At the height of its power, IS controls an area roughly the size of the United Kingdom.

November 2015: IS fighters carry out a coordinated series of attacks in Paris, killing 130 people. These and other attacks in Europe, the Middle East and Africa are increasing global attention and intensifying international efforts to fight ISIS.

2016: International coalition forces and local militias (such as the Iraqi army, the Kurdish Peshmerga, and the Syrian Democratic Forces) launch large-scale military operations against ISIS. IS is losing important cities such as Fallujah and Dabiq.

July 2017: After months of fighting, Iraqi forces recapture Mosul, which is a decisive blow to IS.
October 2017: The Syrian Democratic Forces (SDF), supported by US-led airstrikes, capture Raqqa, the former capital of the IS caliphate.

December 2018: IS is pushed back further in Syria and Iraq and only controls small isolated areas.

March 2019: The SDF captures the last ISIS area in Baghuz, Syria. This marks the de facto end of the territorial "caliphate".
October 2019: Abu Bakr al-Baghdadi is killed in a US-led military operation in Syria. This is a serious symbolic blow to ISIS, although the organization remains active and maintains terrorist cells in various countries.

2020-present: ISIS continues to operate as an underground movement in Syria, Iraq and other regions. Despite the loss of the "caliphate", IS remains a threat, especially through attacks and guerrilla tactics in unstable regions.

BUILDING THE ISLAMIC STATE

The construction of the Islamic State is the result of a complex mixture of religious ideology, military organization and state structure. ISIS has emerged as a hybrid entity that acts as both a terrorist organization and a proto-state entity.

ISIS developed a complex political structure that represents an attempt to establish an Islamic state according to Sharia principles. This structure is based on a centralized management model, supported by hierarchical management.

At the head of IS was the caliph, Abu Bakr al-Baghdadi, who acted as the highest religious and political authority. He was responsible for various councils and committees, each of which controlled different areas of the administration and the military. The most important committees included:

Shura Council: This council consisted of the caliph's closest advisors and had an advisory function in religious and political matters.
Military Council: This council was responsible for planning and conducting military operations.
Sharia Council: The Sharia Council monitored the observance of Sharia law and decided on religious and legal matters.

ISIS divided the areas under its control into different provinces (Wilayat), each of which was headed by a governor (Wali). The

Wilayat were divided into smaller districts, which allowed for local administration. This structure was designed to exercise effective control over the occupied territories while enforcing the ideological doctrine of ISIS.

ISIS developed a highly organized and efficient military structure that included both conventional and unconventional warfare. ISIS's military strength has been a key factor in its ability to capture and control large areas in Iraq and Syria.

ISIS's military units consisted of regular fighters and elite special units. The regular armed forces were made up of experienced fighters and recruits who came from different parts of the world. The elite units, such as the "Inghimasi" (suicide fighters), were used for particularly dangerous and strategic missions.

ISIS combined traditional guerrilla tactics with modern military strategies to defeat its opponents. Preferred methods included asymmetric warfare, the use of improvised explosive devices (IEDs), suicide bombings, and the use of social media for psychological warfare.

IS has been able to capture a considerable amount of modern weapons and equipment by conquering military bases and weapons depots, especially in Iraq. These included tanks, artillery, rocket launchers and even anti-aircraft systems. This equipment gave ISIS a significant military advantage in the early stages of its rise.

ISIS relied on rigorous social control and a sophisticated propaganda strategy to consolidate its power and spread its ideology.

A strict surveillance and judicial system have been established in the areas controlled by ISIS. The "Hisbah" (religious police) monitored the observance of Sharia law and punished violations, while special courts that judge according to Sharia law dealt with cases of deviation or opposition quickly and brutally.

So far, IS has only changed leadership through the death of the previous leader.

- 05/2010 – 10/2019: Abū Bakr al-Baghdādī
- 11/2019 – 02/2022: Abu Ibrahim al-Hashimi al-Qurayshi
- 03/2022 – 11/2022: Abu Hassan al-Hashimi al-Qurayshi
- 11/2022 – 4/2023: Abu al-Husayn al-Husaini al-Quraishi
- from 08/2023: Abu Hafs al-Hashimi al-Qurashi

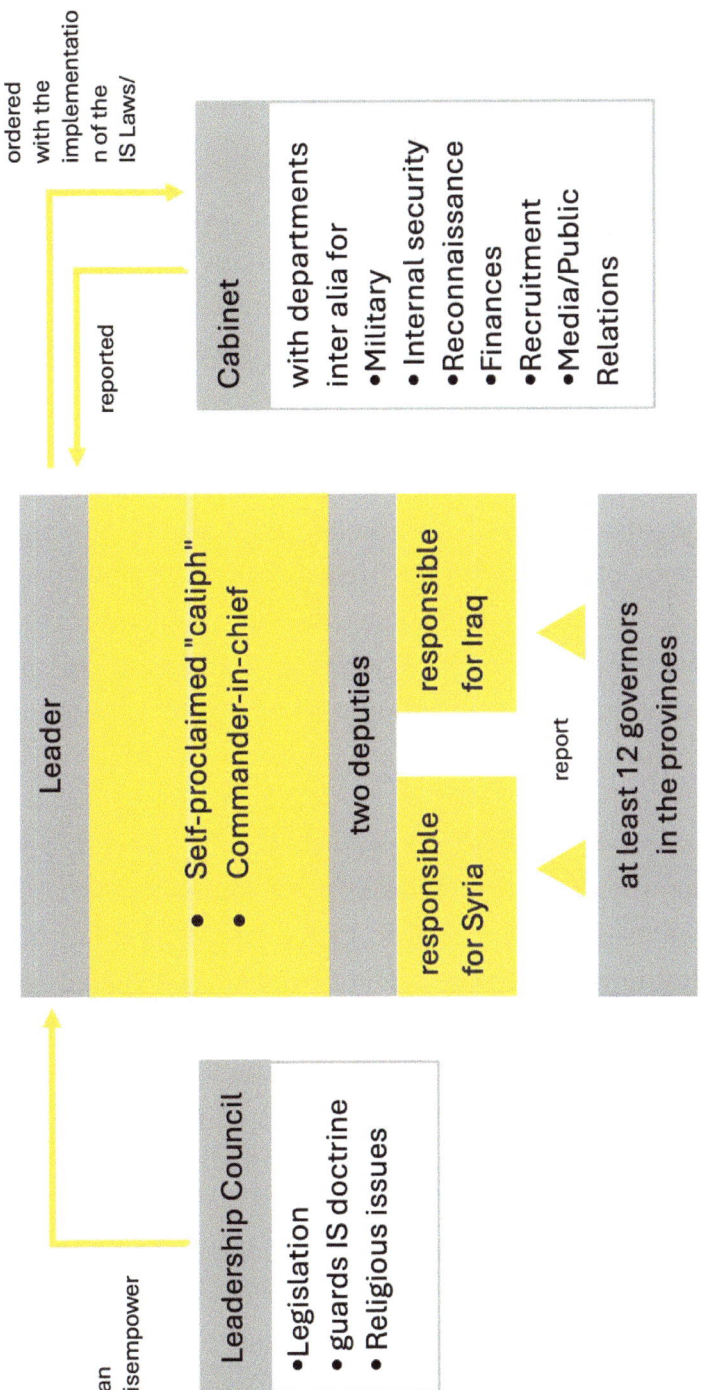

Leadership Council

- Legislation
- guards IS doctrine
- Religious issues

can disempower

Leader

- Self-proclaimed "caliph"
- Commander-in-chief

two deputies

responsible for Syria

responsible for Iraq

at least 12 governors in the provinces

report

ordered with the implementation of the IS Laws/

reported

Cabinet

with departments inter alia for

- Military
- Internal security
- Reconnaissance
- Finances
- Recruitment
- Media/Public Relations

THE RISE OF RADICAL ISLAMISM

Radical Islamism is a political and religious phenomenon that gained much importance in the second half of the 20th century. Its origins are deeply rooted in the history of Islam, but its modern form is the result of a complex interplay of colonialism, political oppression, social inequality, ideological conflicts, and geopolitical influences.

The term "Islamism" refers to political movements that consider Islam to be a comprehensive basis for the organization of society and the state. In contrast to traditional Islam, which focuses primarily on personal piety, Islamism strives to establish Islam as a political ideology. Radical Islamism is an extreme form of Islamism that often supports violent means to achieve its goals.

Important ideological roots of Islamism lie in the early 20th century, especially in the writings of intellectuals such as Hassan al-Banna and Sayyid Qutb, the founders of the Muslim Brotherhood. Qutb's writings, especially "milestones," influenced a generation of Islamists and laid the foundation for the idea that the Muslim world must be liberated through armed jihad from Western domination perceived as corrupt and secular regimes, which are considered un-Islamic.

A major factor in the rise of radical Islamism was the end of European colonialism in the Muslim world. Colonial rule, especially by Britain and France, led to profound social and political changes in many Muslim countries. Traditional structures were shattered, and many Muslim societies faced Western values, secularism, and economic exploitation. Colonial oppression left a deep sense of humiliation and cultural loss that caused many Muslims to long for a return to Islamic values and traditions.

After the end of colonialism, many newly independent Muslim states came under the control of secular, authoritarian regimes, often supported by Western powers. These regimes, such as that of Gamal Abdel Nasser in Egypt or that of Reza Pahlavi in Iran, brutally suppressed Islamist movements and thus created a breeding ground for radical ideas. Disappointment with the post-colonial order and growing dissatisfaction with social inequality and corruption in many of these countries led to more and more people turning to Islamism.

The rise of radical Islamism is closely linked to geopolitical developments during the Cold War. The rivalry between the U.S. and the Soviet Union played a central role in creating the conditions that fostered radicalism.

A key event was the Soviet invasion of Afghanistan in 1979. As part of the Cold War, the US, Saudi Arabia and Pakistan supported the Afghan Mujahideen, an Islamist resistance movement that fought against the Soviet occupation. This support included financial resources, arms deliveries and the training of fighters. In this context, a transnational Islamist movement emerged that propagated the idea of armed jihad as a

legitimate means of defending Islam. The U.S. role in supporting the Mujahideen, including the later leaders of al-Qaeda,
shows the complex and often paradoxical dynamics of geopolitical interests that helped strengthen radical Islamism.

Another decisive event was the Islamic Revolution in Iran in
1979. The revolution overthrew the secular, Western-oriented
regime of the Shah and led to the establishment of an Islamic
state under the leadership of Ayatollah Khomeini. This revolution had enormous symbolic significance for Islamists worldwide, as it showed that it was possible to overthrow a secular
regime and establish a government based on Islamic principles.

Khomeini's revolution, however, was Shiite, while most Islamist movements are Sunni. Nevertheless, it had a strong influence on the radical Islamist movements, as it legitimized jihad
as a means of eliminating un-Islamic rule and revived the idea
of an Islamic state.

Another central role in the rise of radical Islamism was played
by Saudi Arabia, which since the 1970s has invested billions
of dollars in the export of Wahhabism, an ultra-conservative
interpretation of Islam. By building mosques, funding schools,
and supporting Islamist groups, Saudi Arabia helped spread
Wahhabi ideology around the world, especially in regions
such as Southeast Asia, Africa, and Europe. This ideology,
which calls for strict adherence to Sharia law and considers

other interpretations of Islam to be heresy, formed the basis for many radical Islamist movements.

The first Gulf War in 1990-1991, in which a US-led coalition ousted Saddam Hussein's Iraq from Kuwait, also had a profound impact on radical Islamism. Many Islamists regarded the stationing of American troops on Saudi Arabian soil, the land of Islam's two holiest sites, as a grave insult. Osama bin Laden, the leader of al-Qaeda, cited this fact as one of the main reasons for his jihad against the US. The Gulf War helped to stir up anti-Western resentment in the Muslim world and strengthen radical groups.

Globalization and modernization have also influenced radical Islamism. Rapid economic and technological progress, often perceived as "Western", led to social and cultural change in many Muslim countries. Many people felt threatened by the rapid change in their traditional ways of life and sought refuge in religious movements that propagated a return to the "true" values of Islam.

Globalization also facilitated the spread of radical ideas. The internet and social media enabled Islamist groups to spread their ideologies worldwide and recruit new followers. This development contributed significantly to the formation of transnational networks of radical Islamism.

ISIS'S IDEOLOGY: AN ANALYSIS OF RELIGIOUS EXTREMISM

The Islamic State, also known as the Islamic State in Iraq and Syria (ISIS) or the Islamic State of Iraq and the Levant (ISIL), has established itself as one of the most brutal and radical jihadist groups of modern times. Although ISIS attracted worldwide attention in 2014 due to its rapid territorial growth and extreme violence, its ideological roots have a deeper and more complex history. ISIS's ideology is a mixture of religious extremism, political totalitarianism, and military jihad, based on a radical interpretation of Islam.

The ideology of IS is based on an ultra-conservative, puritanical interpretation of Sunni Islam, especially Salafism and Wahhabism. These currents demand a literal interpretation of Islamic texts – the Koran and the Hadith – and reject any innovations (bid'ah) in religious practice that emerged after the time of the Prophet Muhammad. However, IS goes far beyond traditional Salafism by using violent means and rigid totalitarianism to enforce its vision of a "true" Islamic state.

ISIS sees itself as the only legitimate representative of Islam and condemns all other Islamic sects, especially Shiites, as well as other Sunni groups that do not subscribe to its interpretation of the faith. This manifests itself in the ideological justification for mass murders of Shiites, Yazidis, Christians and other religious minorities. ISIS justifies such acts through

24

a selective reading of Islamic sources, selecting specific texts as the basis for its violence, ignoring other aspects of Islamic doctrine that emphasize peace and tolerance.

A central element of the IS ideology is the claim to restore the caliphate. In the Islamic tradition, the caliph is the successor of the Prophet Muhammad and the leader of the entire Muslim community (ummah). The caliphate was officially abolished by the Turkish government in 1924 with the dissolution of the Ottoman Empire, which many Islamist thinkers saw as a symbolic loss of the political and religious unity of Islam.

The proclamation of the caliphate by IS in June 2014 was not only a propaganda move, but an ideological signal that IS intends to restore the historical and divinely sanctioned order. By restoring the caliphate, ISIS sought to unite the Muslim people into a global unity under one Islamic leader, claiming to represent and guide all Muslims worldwide. The caliph of ISIS, Abu Bakr al-Baghdadi, declared that all Muslims owe him obedience, which was a clear break with the modern nation-states and political orders in the Islamic world.

ISIS relies heavily on the concept of jihad, which has various meanings in the Islamic tradition, from spiritual battles to the military defense of Islam. However, ISIS focuses exclusively on military jihad as the main means of achieving its goals. In the ideology of ISIS, jihad is not only an option, but a duty for all Muslims. ISIS defines jihad as a holy war against all those who do not follow its extreme interpretation of Islam – both non-Muslims and apostate Muslims (takfir).

The concept of takfir plays a central role in ISIS ideology. It refers to the practice of declaring other Muslims to be infidels if they do not follow the strict teachings of ISIS. ISIS uses takfir to legitimize its attacks on other Muslims, including the mass murder of Shiites, Sufis, and even Sunni Muslims who do not accept ISIS's strict discipline. This practice contradicts traditional Islamic rules, which prescribe great restraint in the use of takfir.

In addition to the idea of caliphate and jihad, apocalyptic messianism plays an important role in the ideology of IS. The leadership of ISIS interprets certain Islamic texts to mean that ISIS has a divine mission to prepare for the end times. These apocalyptic notions are particularly linked to the hadith, which describes the battle of Dabiq, a small town in Syria, as the scene of a decisive confrontation between Muslims and infidels that is supposed to precede the coming of the Mahdi (a Messianic leader) and the Last Judgment.

ISIS used this apocalyptic vision as a propaganda tool to motivate and recruit its followers by claiming that they were part of a divine plan that would lead to the final restoration of justice in the world. This eschatological dimension also helped to justify the extreme violence of ISIS, as it was seen as a necessary means to realize the divine plan.

Another central component of ISIS's ideology is the enforcement of Sharia, Islamic law, which ISIS interprets in its most extreme and rigorous form. ISIS considers Sharia law to be the only valid legal system and applies it brutally and without regard for contextual differences. This includes corporal punishment such as amputations and flogging, executions of homosexuals and adulterers, and the enslavement of women, especially those considered "infidels."

ISIS's strict application of Sharia law is part of its broader ideology, which includes the rejection of modern institutions and laws, especially Western secularization and democracy. For IS, democracy is an un-Islamic invention, as it replaces the rule of God with the rule of the people. IS rejects all forms of the rule of law that are not based on its extreme interpretation of Sharia.

THE ORIGIN OF JIHADISM: FROM SAYYID QUTB TO AL-QAEDA

The term "jihadism" refers to a radical ideology that justifies armed struggle as a means of spreading and defending Islam. The modern jihadist movement, which is now most associated with organizations such as Al-Qaeda and the Islamic State (IS). A key figure in this development was the Egyptian Islamist Sayyid Qutb, whose ideas laid the foundation for modern jihadism.

Sayyid Qutb (1906–1966) was an Egyptian writer, teacher and a leading thinker of the Muslim Brotherhood. His writings, especially "Ma'alim fi al-Tariq" (Signs on the Way), have had a profound effect on the development of modern Islamist thought.

Qutb considered the world to be in a state of "Jahiliyya," a term that originally referred to "ignorance" before the revelation of Islam. However, he used the term to describe the modern world, which he believed was steeped in materialism, moral decadence, and a lack of divine guidance. Qutb argued that the Muslim community (ummah) must be freed from this "jahiliyya" and that this can only be done by returning to a pure, authentic Islam.

A central aspect of Qutb's thought was the conception of jihad as a "defensive" war against the forces of infidelity and oppression. While jihad was primarily understood in traditional Islamic law as a collective duty (fard kifaya) that should only be exercised under certain conditions and in a specific context, Qutb expanded the meaning of the term. For him, jihad was not only a physical but also an ideological obligation, with the aim of restoring the Islamic order and fighting against those who threatened it.

Qutb's ideas resonated with a new generation of Islamists in the 1960s, who were radicalized by growing frustration with Western domination, the colonial past, and the lack of authority of Muslim states. Especially in Egypt, where Qutb himself was imprisoned and eventually executed under the repressive regime of Gamal Abdel Nasser, his writings developed a strong attraction for radical Islamists.

In the decades that followed, Qutb's ideas contributed to the emergence of several radical Islamist groups that took up armed struggle against their own governments and against the West. Among the best-known groups are the Egyptian Islamic Jihad (EIJ) and Al-Jamaa al-Islamiyya, which were active in Egypt in the 1970s and 1980s.

The development of global jihadism, as represented by Al-Qaeda, cannot be fully understood without the influence of Qutb. A key event in the history of modern jihadism was the Soviet invasion of Afghanistan in 1979. This event mobilized thousands of Muslims from all over the world who joined the "jihad" against the Soviet occupation.

Among these fighters was Osama bin Laden, a Saudi multimillionaire who later founded Al-Qaeda. Bin Laden and his associates viewed the success of the Afghan jihad as proof of the power of armed resistance and the possibility of achieving greater goals, including the expulsion of Western powers from Muslim countries and the establishment of a caliphate.

While Qutb laid the ideological foundation, it was bin Laden who translated these ideas into a global movement. The doctrine of "distant enemies," as advocated by al-Qaeda, expanded the enemy images from local regimes to global powers, especially the United States and its allies. This eventually led to the terrorist attacks of September 11, 2001, which changed the face of global terrorism and ushered the world into the "era of terrorism."

ISIS AND THE QUESTION OF "HOLY WAR": RELIGIOUS JUSTIFICATIONS AND THEIR CONTRADICTIONS

The "holy war", or jihad, is one of the central concepts in the ideology of the Islamic State (IS). ISIS has instrumentalized the concept of jihad to justify its brutal military campaigns, acts of terrorism and the creation of an Islamic caliphate. The group claims that its actions are in line with the teachings of Islam and are a necessary step towards restoring a "pure" Islamic order. Nevertheless, there are many debates within the Islamic community and among scholars about whether ISIS's interpretation and use of jihad is legitimate.

In Islam, jihad literally means "effort" or "struggle" and has different meanings depending on the context. There are two main forms of jihad: the "great jihad" (al-jihād al-akbar) and the "small jihad" (al-jihād al-asghar). The great jihad refers to the inner spiritual struggle of a Muslim to purify his soul and live a life in harmony with God's commandments. The small jihad, on the other hand, refers to the physical struggle to defend Islam, which is considered justified under certain conditions, such as when Muslims are attacked or oppressed.

Historically, the meaning of small-scale jihad has changed over the centuries. In classical Islamic jurisprudence, military jihad is primarily seen as defensive and must follow certain ethical norms and conditions. For example, it may only be declared under the authority of a legitimate ruler and must respect the distinction between combatants and non-combatants.

ISIS has redefined jihad in a particularly radical and aggressive form. For ISIS, jihad is not just a defensive measure, but an offensive duty for all Muslims aimed at restoring Islamic rule globally. IS bases its legitimacy on certain Koran suras and hadiths, which it believes justify the armed struggle against infidels and apostate Muslims. ISIS often quotes the Qur'anic verse 9:5, known as the "sword verse": *"And when the holy months are over, kill the polytheists wherever you find them...".*

IS interprets this and other verses as a universal call for militant struggle against all those who do not submit to its extreme interpretation of Islam. However, this interpretation is in sharp contrast to traditional interpretations of jihad, which place the "sword verse" in the historical context of the early Islamic wars against the polytheists in Mecca and do not see it as a universally applicable guideline.

A central element in the legitimation of jihad by IS is the concept of **takfir.** Takfir refers to the practice of declaring other Muslims to be infidels, making them legitimate targets in battle. ISIS has taken this practice to the extreme, using it to demonize Muslims who do not follow its interpretation of Islam. This includes not only Shiite Muslims, who are considered heretics by ISIS, but also Sunni Muslims who refuse to recognize the rule of the caliphate or submit to ISIS's strict laws.

The practice of takfir is highly controversial within the Islamic tradition. Many Islamic scholars warn against using takfir prematurely, as it can lead to division and chaos in the Muslim community. The indiscriminate use of takfir by ISIS is in direct contradiction to these precautions and is considered illegitimate by most Islamic scholars.

ISIS's religious justifications are based on a selective and contextually distorted interpretation of Islamic texts. While ISIS invokes certain Quranic verses and hadiths to justify its actions, it also ignores Islam's broader ethical and legal principles that limit violence and emphasize the protection of civilians. A classic example of these contradictions is the question of the distinction between combatants and non-combatants.

The Islamic martial law tradition places great emphasis on the protection of non-combatants, especially women, children, the elderly, and religious minorities. The Prophet Muhammad himself established rules for dealing with enemies in war, prohibiting, for example, the killing of women and children and the wanton destruction of property and infrastructure. ISIS, however, has completely overridden these principles by carrying out targeted attacks on civilians, including mass executions, suicide bombings, and the enslavement of women and children. Such acts are contrary to the ethical precepts of Sharia law and have led to fierce criticism from Islamic scholars worldwide.

ISIS uses jihad not only as a religious duty, but also as a political tool. ISIS's "holy war" aims to destabilize existing political structures and create a theocratic order based on the extremist interpretation of Sharia law. IS legitimizes its attacks on Western states and governments in the Muslim world by portraying them as un-Islamic and corrupt, influenced by the West and thus illegitimate. ISIS's political motives are obscured by the religious rhetoric of jihad, which allows the group to mobilize followers who believe in the spiritual and eschatological dimensions of the struggle.

ISIS's strategy is to create an atmosphere of fear and chaos that makes its rule appear to be the only solution for restoring order and justice. At the same time, ISIS uses the symbolism of "holy war" to commit its followers to a total and uncompromising commitment to its goals, which explains the extreme brutality and fanaticism that characterizes the group.

While ISIS claims to be the true representative of Islam, there is significant resistance from the Islamic world to its ideology and practice. Numerous prominent Islamic scholars have published fatwas and statements condemning ISIS as illegitimate and un-Islamic. The Amman Message, an initiative of Islamic scholars that condemns the abuse of Islamic teachings by extremists, explicitly contradicts the practice of takfir and emphasizes the unity of the Muslim community.

Moreover, both Sunni and Shiite scholars have criticized ISIS for abusing the notion of jihad, turning it into a universal call to war that distorts the foundations of Islam. Al-Azhar University in Cairo, one of the most respected institutions of Sunni Islam, has repeatedly stated that ISIS's actions are incompatible with the teachings of Islam and that ISIS does not have the authority to proclaim the caliphate or declare jihad.

THE DISINTEGRATION OF IRAQ AND THE BIRTH OF THE ISLAMIC STATE

The disintegration of Iraq and the emergence of the "Islamic State" (IS) are among the most significant events in the recent history of the Middle East. This development was the result of a complex mix of political, social and military factors that worked together over several decades. The collapse of state institutions, deep-rooted ethnic and religious tensions, and the intervention of external powers all helped to create an environment in which ISIS could rise.

To understand the disintegration of Iraq, one must look at the political and social structure of the country before 2003. Iraq was a state marked by deep ethnic and sectarian tensions. The three main groups – the Shiite Arabs, the Sunni Arabs and the Kurds – were often in a tense relationship with each other. Since the end of the First World War and the establishment of the modern Iraqi state by the British Mandate, the country has been marked by a constant power struggle between these groups.

The rule of the Baath Party, especially under Saddam Hussein, increased these tensions. Saddam's Sunni regime suppressed the Shiite majority and the Kurdish minority with brutal violence, which led to a deep division within Iraqi society. Despite these internal tensions, however, Iraq remained a functioning state, albeit authoritarian and repressive.

The US-led invasion of Iraq in 2003 marked a turning point in the country's history. The fall of Saddam Hussein led to a power vacuum, which was exacerbated by the rapid collapse of state institutions. The decision of the US administration to disband the Iraqi army and remove members of the Baath Party from public life (so-called "de-Baathification") left the country without a functioning government and led to the alienation and radicalization of many Sunnis, who suddenly found themselves without power and prospects.

The following years were marked by a bloody civil war between Sunni and Shiite militias. The Shiite-dominated government formed after the first democratic elections was seen by many Sunnis as illegitimate and sectarian. These tensions were further exacerbated by the intervention of external actors, notably Iran, which supported Shiite militias, and the US, which sought to stabilize the new government.

It was in this chaotic environment that the group that would later become known as the Islamic State (IS) emerged. The origin of IS lies in the Jordanian terrorist group al-Tawhid wal-Jihad, which was founded in 1999 by Abu Musab al-Zarqawi. This group later joined Al-Qaeda and operated under the name Al-Qaeda in Iraq (AQI). Al-Zarqawi's group has been responsible for some of the bloodiest attacks in Iraq since 2003, including numerous suicide bombings against Shiite civilians that further fueled sectarian conflict.

After al-Zarqawi's death in 2006 and the merger of various Sunni groups, the "Islamic State in Iraq" (ISI) was founded. This group saw itself as the pioneer of a Sunni uprising against the Shiite-dominated Iraqi government and the US occupation. Nevertheless, the ISI remained a marginal phenomenon for a long time, until the geopolitical landscape in the Middle East changed again.

The outbreak of the civil war in Syria in 2011 provided an opportunity for the ISI to expand its power. The Syrian crisis created a power vacuum like that in Iraq, and the ISI used this to entrench itself in the uncontrolled areas of Syria. In 2013, the group announced the establishment of the "Islamic State in Iraq and the Levant" (ISIL or ISIS) under its new leader Abu Bakr al-Baghdadi.

ISIS benefited from the weakness of the Syrian government and increasing radicalization in opposition-controlled areas. The group quickly conquered territories and gained influence through its brutality and sophisticated propaganda strategies. The capture of the Iraqi city of Mosul in June 2014 marked the culmination of this rise. Al-Baghdadi then proclaimed the caliphate and changed the name of the group to "Islamic State" (IS).

The disintegration of the Iraqi state and the birth of ISIS were closely linked to the mistakes of US policy and the sectarian policies of the Iraqi government. The exclusion of Sunni Arabs from political power and the marginalization of their communities created the breeding ground for the rise of radical groups such as ISIS. The withdrawal of US troops in 2011, without a stable political order having been established in Iraq, increased the power vacuum and allowed ISIS to present itself as the defender of the Sunni community.

Iran also played an ambivalent role by supporting Shiite militias, which fought effectively against ISIS, but also further fueled sectarian tensions. Turkish policy, which has long supported Islamist groups in Syria, and the hesitant attitude of Western powers also contributed to the complexity of the conflict.

THE RISE OF ABU BAKR AL-BAGHDADI: FROM SHADOW MAN TO CALIPH

Abu Bakr al-Baghdadi, born Ibrahim Awwad Ibrahim al-Badri al-Samarrai, became known worldwide as the leader of the "Islamic State" (IS). His rise from a largely unknown preacher to a self-proclaimed "caliph" marks a pivotal moment in the history of global jihadism. Al-Baghdadi skillfully exploited the political, social,

and religious tensions in Iraq and Syria to form one of the most brutal and influential terrorist organizations in modern history.

Abu Bakr al-Baghdadi was born in 1971 in the city of Samarra, north of Baghdad. His family belonged to Sunni Arabism, and it is claimed that his ancestry can be traced back to the Prophet Muhammad, which earned him special respect in traditional Islamic societies. Al-Baghdadi grew up in a time of significant political and social upheaval that shaped Iraq.

He studied Islamic theology at the University of Baghdad and earned a doctorate in Islamic studies with a focus on Quranic studies and Sharia. This academic training gave him a deep knowledge of Islamic law and theology, which later helped him legitimize his role as a religious leader of ISIS.

Al-Baghdadi's entry into radical Islamism was gradual. In the 1990s, he joined jihadist circles, but he remained largely in the background. However, Iraq's political landscape changed drastically after the US-led invasion in 2003. The overthrow of Saddam Hussein and the subsequent occupation led to a power vacuum and a wave of violence that al-Baghdadi and many other radicalized Sunnis saw as an opportunity to expand their influence.

During this time, al-Baghdadi became a member of Al-Qaeda in Iraq (AQI), a group founded by Abu Musab al-Zarqawi. Zarqawi's AQI was known for its extreme brutality and hatred of Shiites, which contributed to the escalation of sectarian conflict in Iraq. After al-Zarqawi's death in 2006, the group was renamed the Islamic State of Iraq (ISI).

After the deaths of several ISI leaders in 2006 and 2010, al-Baghdadi quickly rose through the group's hierarchy. In 2010, he finally took over the leadership of the ISI. Under his leadership, the group began to expand its activities and become better organized. Al-Baghdadi placed great emphasis on the ISI being perceived not only as a terrorist group, but as a kind of proto-state capable of exercising territorial control and enforcing a strict Islamic legal system.

A decisive turning point in al-Baghdadi's strategy came with the outbreak of the civil war in Syria in 2011. The conflict provided an opportunity for the ISI to spread in Syria and gain new recruits and resources. Al-Baghdadi sent fighters to Syria in 2013 and declared the establishment of the "Islamic State in Iraq and the Levant" (ISIL or ISIS). This led to tensions with other jihadist groups in the region, especially with the Syrian Al-Nusra Front, which declared itself loyal to Al-Qaeda. However, al-Baghdadi claimed that his organization represented the true successor to al-Qaeda, which led to an open break with the al-Qaeda leadership.

The climax of al-Baghdadi's rise came in June 2014, when his fighters captured the Iraqi city of Mosul, the country's second-largest city. This victory shocked the world and led to the proclamation of the caliphate by al-Baghdadi, who proclaimed himself "Caliph Ibrahim". He made a public appearance in a mosque in Mosul and called on Muslims worldwide to swear allegiance to him.

The proclamation of the caliphate was a significant moment in the modern history of jihadism. Al-Baghdadi thus claimed leadership over the entire Muslim world, based on the claim to restore an Islamic empire that would be governed in accordance with the teachings of the Prophet Muhammad and his early successors. This move gave ISIS an unprecedented appeal, attracting thousands of jihadists from all over the world who flocked to the so-called "caliphate" to fight for al-Baghdadi.

Under al-Baghdadi's leadership, ISIS experienced a period of aggressive expansion and extreme violence. The group conquered large parts of Iraq and Syria and established a brutal regime based on a strict interpretation of Sharia law. Public executions, mass murders, enslavements, and other atrocities were commonplace. Al-Baghdadi and his followers deliberately relied on the shock effect of their violence to spread fear and consolidate their power.

ISIS also used modern means of communication and social media to spread its propaganda worldwide. This strategy helped the group gain a global following and inspire attacks outside the Middle East. Al-Baghdadi's image as an intrepid and unyielding leader has been carefully cultivated, although he himself rarely appeared in public.

Despite its rapid rise, IS began to be under military pressure from 2015 onwards. An international coalition led by the United States, as well as the armed forces of Syria, Iraq and Kurdish militias, launched a series of counter-offensives that gradually pushed IS out of its strongholds. By 2019, IS had lost almost all its territorial conquests.

On October 27, 2019, Abu Bakr al-Baghdadi was killed in the US military operation Kayla Mueller in the Syrian province of Idlib. His death was hailed as a significant victory in the fight against ISIS, although the ideology and networks he had created remained. Al-Baghdadi's succession within ISIS remained controversial, and the group was forced to go underground while trying to regroup.

THE CONQUEST OF MOSUL: A TURNING POINT IN THE MIDDLE EAST

The conquest of Mosul by the Islamic State (IS) in June 2014 marked a significant turning point in the history of the Middle East. Mosul, Iraq's second-largest city, fell into the hands of the jihadists surprisingly quickly and became a symbol of the failure of the Iraqi government and the international community to recognize and combat the threat of ISIS in time. The capture of Mosul led to far-reaching consequences: it significantly strengthened ISIS, exacerbated instability in the region and changed the geopolitical landscape of the Middle East.

After the fall of Saddam Hussein in 2003 and the occupation of the country by the United States, Iraq entered a period of severe political instability and sectarian violence. The Shiite-dominated government of Nouri al-Maliki, which came to power after the first democratic elections, pursued a policy of marginalizing the Sunni population, which had previously been the privileged group under Saddam Hussein.

This political exclusion and systematic discrimination led to deep discontent among the Sunnis, who became increasingly alienated from the central government in Baghdad. In this environment, ISIS, which had its origins in the al-Qaeda network, found fertile ground for its ideology. Under the leadership of Abu Bakr al-Baghdadi, ISIS took advantage of the power vacuum and widespread discontent to expand its following and military capabilities.

In 2014, ISIS experienced a period of rapidly growing strength. The civil war in Syria, which had been raging since 2011, had allowed IS to establish itself in the uncontrolled areas of Syria and from there expand its operations into Iraq. At the beginning of 2014, ISIS had already captured several cities in Iraq's Anbar province, including Fallujah, an emblematic city that had been the scene of fierce fighting during the Iraq war.

On June 4, 2014, IS began an offensive on Mosul, the capital of Nineveh province. The offensive came as a surprise to the Iraqi armed forces, and within days the city had fallen. On June 10, 2014, ISIS declared complete control of Mosul. The capture of the city proceeded surprisingly quickly and was favored by the poor moral and organizational conditions of the Iraqi army. Reports say that the Iraqi soldiers fled in panic, some of them took off their uniforms and left their weapons behind, while IS took over the city almost unhindered.

The conquest of Mosul was greeted with shock and disbelief by the international community. The fact that a small group of ISIS fighters was able to take such a significant city of millions was a clear sign of the failure of the Iraqi security forces and the government of Prime Minister al-Maliki. Even more significantly, when ISIS captured Mosul, it captured huge quantities of weapons and military equipment left behind by fleeing Iraqi forces. These included heavy weapons, armored vehicles, and even U.S.-made Humvees, which significantly increased ISIS's military clout.

Shortly after the conquest of Mosul, Abu Bakr al-Baghdadi announced the establishment of a caliphate on June 29, 2014, and proclaimed himself "Caliph Ibrahim". This happened in the Great Mosque of al-Nuri in Mosul, which made the city the symbolic center of the newly proclaimed "Islamic State". With the proclamation of the caliphate, al-Baghdadi claimed leadership not only over the global jihadist movement, but also over the entire Muslim world, based on the claim to restore the "proper" Islamic state.

The proclamation of the caliphate was an important propaganda tool for IS. It attracted thousands of jihadists from all over the world who poured into Mosul and other areas controlled by ISIS. ISIS presented itself as the defender of Sunni Islam against what it saw as Shiite oppression and Western interference, which further strengthened its appeal in the Sunni world.

The capture of Mosul had a profound impact on the regional and global security situation. ISIS's ability to control such an important city and declare a caliphate posed an unprecedented threat to stability in the Middle East. Mosul became the administrative and military center of ISIS, from where the group continued its expansion in both Iraq and Syria.

The capture of Mosul also had devastating humanitarian consequences. Hundreds of thousands of people fled the city, while those who remained suffered under the brutal rule of ISIS. ISIS introduced a rigid interpretation of Sharia law in Mosul and other occupied territories, with public executions, torture and enslavement of minorities such as the Yazidis. The destruction of cultural sites, including the Great Mosque of al-Nuri, and the systematic exploitation of resources by IS further exacerbated the suffering of the population.

Internationally, the conquest of Mosul led to increased military intervention against IS. The U.S. and its allies began airstrikes on ISIS positions, while at the same time trying to strengthen local partners such as the Iraqi army and Kurdish Peshmerga militias. The formation of an international coalition against ISIS was directly motivated by the fall of Mosul and the subsequent proclamation of the caliphate.

Although ISIS made considerable territorial gains after the capture of Mosul, its power base began to erode from 2015 onwards. The Iraqi armed forces, supported by Kurdish militias and the international coalition, launched a series of counteroffensives to retake the country. The battle for Mosul, which began in October 2016, became one of the longest and bloodiest battles in the war against ISIS.

In July 2017, the Iraqi government finally announced the complete liberation of Mosul. However, the city was in ruins, and the humanitarian and infrastructural challenges were enormous. The recapture of Mosul marked the end of ISIS's territorial caliphate in Iraq, but the group remained active as a guerrilla movement and a persistent threat to regional stability.

Development of ISIS's territorial control between October 2014 and May 2016

ISIS-controlled areas in Syria and Iraq

Controlled by Syrian rebels

Controlled by the Syrian government

☐ Controlled by al-Nusra Front (Hai at Tahrr al-Sham)

Controlled by the Iraqi government

Controlled by Syrian Kurds

Controlled by Iraqi Kurds

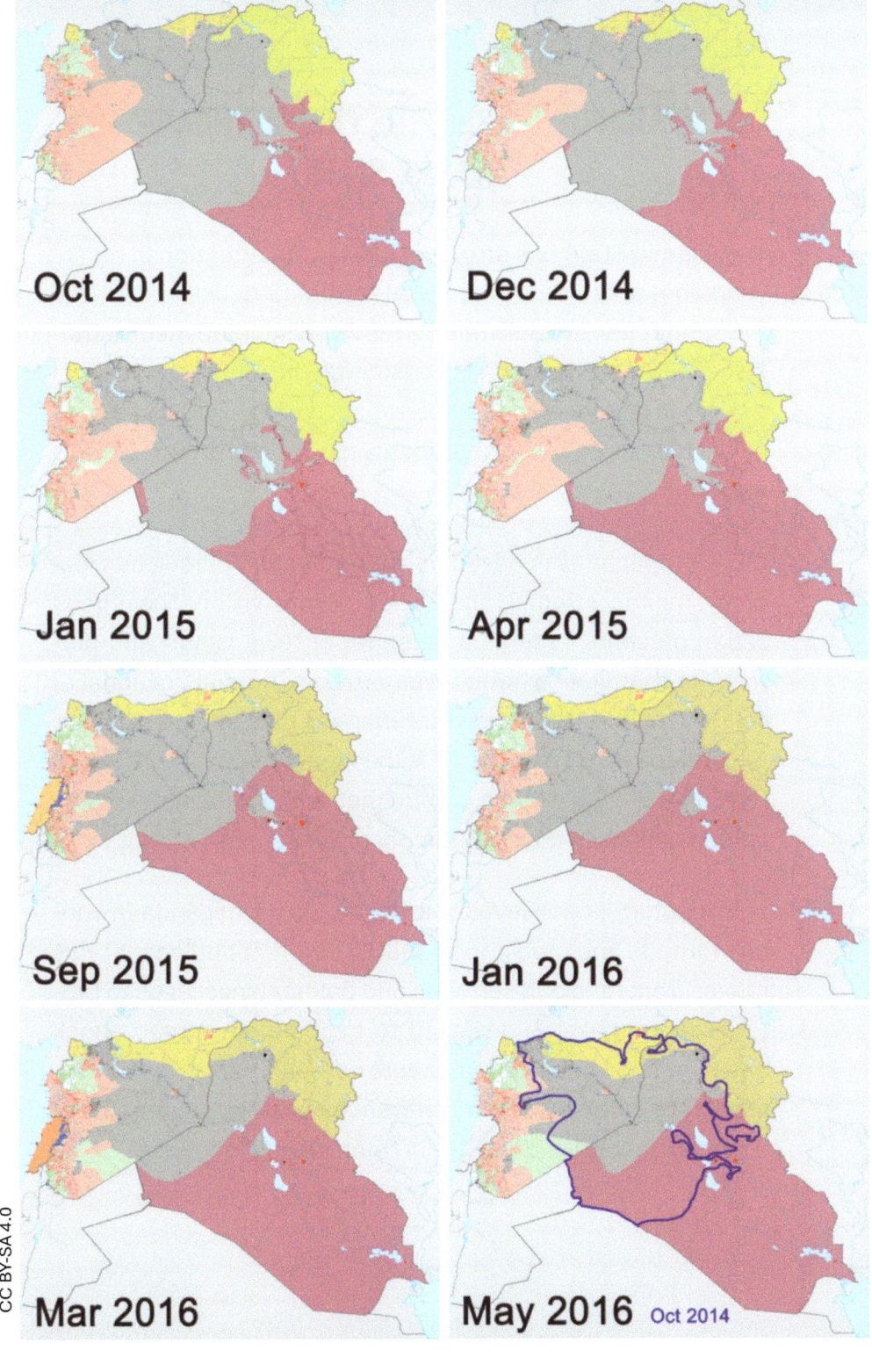

Oct 2014

Dec 2014

Jan 2015

Apr 2015

Sep 2015

Jan 2016

Mar 2016

May 2016   Oct 2014

CAMPAIGN OF TERROR: THE PROPAGANDA OF THE ISLAMIC STATE

The Islamic State has attracted worldwide attention in recent years, not only through its brutal terrorist attacks and territorial conquests, but also through its sophisticated media strategies. ISIS's propaganda is considered one of the most effective in the history of modern terrorism and has allowed the organization to gain a global following, mobilize new recruits and spread fear.

ISIS's propaganda is based on a combination of religious ideology, military strength and an apocalyptic vision. The organization presents itself as a defender of "true Islam" and portrays its enemies – whether Western governments, regional rivals or religious minorities – as enemies of Islam to be fought. Central to ISIS's propaganda is the idea that ISIS has restored the caliphate, an Islamic empire that existed under the rightly guided caliphs in the early history of Islam.

This ideology is conveyed through ISIS's propaganda in various formats and media to appeal to different audiences. This ranges from religious sermons and political messages to brutal execution videos designed to deliberately spread shock and fear. ISIS knows how to create complex narratives that incorporate both historical references and current political events to justify its ideology and motivate its followers.

A central feature of IS propaganda is the high quality of its media productions. IS has invested considerable resources in building a professional media infrastructure. This includes several media departments, including Al-Hayat Media Center, which is responsible for the production of propaganda videos, magazines and other publications. ISIS's videos feature professional camera work, carefully selected music, and thoughtful staging that depicts the group's brutality in a way designed to evoke both shock and admiration.

An example of this media production is the magazine "Dabiq", which was published in several languages. It was aimed at potential recruits and sympathizers worldwide and conveyed the ideology of ISIS through articles, interviews and reports on ISIS's "successes" on the battlefield. The graphic design and the choice of topics in "Dabiq" and other publications also reflect a deep knowledge of modern communication techniques.

Another key to the success of IS propaganda is the clever use of social networks. ISIS was one of the first terrorist organizations to recognize and use the full potential of platforms such as Twitter, Facebook, YouTube, and later Telegram to spread its messages. Social networks offered IS not only a global reach, but also the opportunity to interact directly with potential followers and recruits.

Particularly striking is the way in which IS used social networks to spread its content virally. ISIS supporters were encouraged to share, comment and redistribute content, leading to a kind of "swarm strategy" in which many accounts spread propaganda at the same time, making it difficult to stop it completely. This strategy allowed ISIS to get its messages to a global audience quickly and effectively, even when individual accounts or videos were deleted from the platforms.

A notable example is the campaign launched by ISIS after the capture of Mosul in June 2014. Within days, the internet was flooded with images, videos, and news of ISIS's "victory," portraying the group as an unstoppable force and attracting potential recruits from around the world.

ISIS's propaganda is characterized by a targeted approach to different target groups. ISIS has recognized that different demographic groups – whether young men in the Middle East, converted Muslims in Europe, or women seeking a role in the "caliphate" – have different motivations and expectations. To do justice to these different groups, IS produces tailor-made content.

For young men, who are often the main target group for military recruitment, ISIS produces videos that glorify the "heroic deeds" of the fighters and glorify martyrdom. These videos combine violent scenes with heroic music and religious quotes to emotionally captivate and radicalize viewers.

For women, ISIS has developed a different kind of propaganda that emphasizes the role of women in the caliphate. This includes content that depicts the "ideal" Muslim wife and mother who lives in the caliphate and raises her children in the spirit of IS. This propaganda aims to encourage women to join ISIS and actively participate in the establishment and maintenance of the caliphate.

ISIS's propaganda is also aimed specifically at Western Muslims, especially those who feel alienated or discriminated against. ISIS is trying to convince these individuals that they will find a "home" and a community in the caliphate that is denied to them in the West. This propaganda deliberately uses frustration and anger over social injustice and discrimination to promote radicalization.

The propaganda of the IS is rich in symbolism and historical references. IS sees itself as the direct successor of the first Islamic caliphate, and this historical connection is repeatedly emphasized in propaganda. The name of the magazine "Dabiq", for example, refers to a prophecy about a decisive battle between Muslims and "infidels" in the Syrian city of Dabiq, which is considered an omen of the end of times and the triumph of Islam.

These recourse to Islamic history is not only intended to increase the legitimacy of ISIS, but also to create an emotional connection with the believers, who should feel motivated by the sense of continuity and historical fate. ISIS uses these narratives to mobilize its fighters and paint a picture of an inevitable victory that is designed to foster hope and perseverance even in times of military defeat and setback.

ISIS's propaganda has far-reaching implications for global security. ISIS's ability to recruit supporters and fighters from around the world has enabled the organization to carry out attacks in different countries and pose a global threat. At the same time, ISIS propaganda has the potential to radicalize lone wolves – individuals who carry out attacks in the name of ISIS without having direct contact with the organization.

This kind of radicalisation poses enormous challenges for the security services. Traditional surveillance and prevention strategies are often not sufficient to prevent the spread of extremist content online or to identify radicalized individuals in a timely manner. In addition, ISIS propaganda has intensified the debate on the role of social networks in the dissemination of extremist content. Many platforms are under increasing pressure to take more effective action against the spread of terrorist propaganda but face the dilemma of balancing freedom of expression and security.

Faced with the threat posed by ISIS propaganda, governments and international organizations have taken various measures to counter the spread of extremist ideas. One of these measures is the increased monitoring and removal of extremist content from social networks. Platforms such as Twitter and Facebook have tightened their policies and are increasingly working with governments to identify and delete terrorist content.

At the same time, there are efforts to develop counterpropaganda designed to undermine ISIS's narratives. These initiatives aim to demystify the "myth" of the caliphate and show the reality of violence and oppression under ISIS rule. Such programs seek to reduce the attractiveness of ISIS, especially for potential recruits, and to identify alternatives that are compatible with the values of Islam without promoting violence and extremism.

RADICALISATION AND RECRUITMENT

The Islamic State (IS) gained global notoriety between 2013 and 2018 for its brutal acts of terrorism, the establishment of a self-proclaimed caliphate, and the recruitment of tens of thousands of foreign fighters. The radicalization and recruitment of individuals worldwide was a central aspect of ISIS's power base and was crucial to the spread of its ideology and military successes.

Radicalisation refers to a process by which individuals develop increasingly extreme views that support or justify violent behavior. In the context of ISIS, radicalization means that people are gradually convinced of the ideology of jihadist Salafism, which sees a violent struggle to establish an Islamic state as a religious duty.

This process is not linear and can take place in different social, political and individual contexts. Radicalization is the result of a complex interplay of factors such as identity crises, political gravamina, social injustices, and individual psychological states. About IS, the alienation of young Muslims in Western societies, marginalization in home countries, traumatic experiences and the attraction of a clearly structured and identity-forming ideology were identified as key factors.

ISIS has created a narrative structure that is appealing on several levels: it offered its followers a clear, albeit distorted, idea of how the Islamic world and global power structures should function. Central to this ideology was the idea that the Muslim world was threatened by "infidels" and "traitors," and that it was the religious duty of every Muslim to ward off these threats, whether through migration to the caliphate or through struggle.

IS combined its messages with apocalyptic ideas and presented itself as the last line of defense of Islam. Particularly appealing to many young men and women was the idea of being part of a cosmic struggle between good and evil and fulfilling a higher spiritual calling. The IS painted a picture of a utopian community in which Muslims could live according to the rules of Sharia law without being hindered by secular or Western influences.

Recruitment by IS was carried out in a variety of ways and was extremely flexible both in terms of the target groups and the means used. IS knew how to combine modern technologies and traditional methods of recruitment to reach different target groups.

Online recruitment and social media: ISIS effectively used modern means of communication such as social networks, messaging services and video portals to reach potential recruits. Professionally produced videos, glossy magazines such as "Dabiq" and "Rumiyah", and social media platforms have been used to spread the ideology, show success stories of fighters, and propagate ISIS's moral superiority over other Islamic groups and Western governments. Young people were targeted by the anonymity and reach of social media, often by personally addressing already radicalized "online recruiters".

Territorial control and physical presence: In the areas it controls in Iraq and Syria, IS relied on a local presence that was not only military in nature, but also included social services, education and administration. This allowed the group to recruit young men and women by promising them both material and ideological security. The creation of a society in which Sharia law applies without restriction was presented to escape the corruption and upheavals of the post-colonial Arab states.

Diaspora networks: ISIS used diaspora networks in Europe, North Africa and Asia to mobilize fighters and supporters. Mosques, community centers and prisons were places where potential recruits were tracked down. ISIS benefited from existing links to Salafist networks that shared similar ideological views and thus served as a springboard for recruitment.

Martyrdom and sacrifice: ISIS's ideology strongly emphasized the concept of martyrdom. Suicide bombers were portrayed as heroes who fulfilled their duty to God. This glorification of death for the cause of God had a strong attraction, especially for young people who were looking for meaning. IS portrayed martyrdom as a direct path to paradise and promised fighters heavenly rewards.

Target group adaptation: IS differentiated its recruitment strategies according to the target group. For Western followers, often young Muslims or converts, questions of identity, discrimination and alienation were in the foreground. In the Arab world, on the other hand, there was a greater focus on issues such as the fight against corrupt governments and Western interference.

The reasons why people were susceptible to the radical ideology of IS are diverse and complex. Social isolation, discrimination, unemployment and lack of prospects play just as much a role as individual factors, such as trauma or family problems.

Identity crises and alienation: Especially in Western countries, IS became attractive to young Muslims who felt alienated from their societies. Experiences of discrimination, Islamophobia and a lack of belonging led to IS being seen as an alternative to a society perceived as hostile. ISIS's ideology offered clear identity features, and a community based on religious principles.

Socio-economic factors: In many countries in the Middle East and North Africa, but also in Western countries, economic factors played an important role. Unemployment, poverty and a lack of educational and prospects created a fertile environment for recruitment by IS. The prospect of a "just" and "safe" life in the caliphate, coupled with a clear image of the enemy, made IS attractive to many people who felt abandoned by the existing political and economic systems.

Psychological factors: Individuals in search of meaning, belonging and structure often proved to be particularly vulnerable to radicalisation by ISIS. The group offered simple answers to complex questions of life and promised a clear order in which personal sacrifices for the collective good were glorified. Often it was young men who identified with a toxic form of masculinity who saw jihad to prove their masculinity.
The radicalization to IS did not follow fixed patterns but was a dynamic and individual process. Some recruits were radicalized in a short period of time, while others took years to process. IS used this individual approach to adapt to different psychological and social needs. The role of social networks and peer groups is particularly striking: radicalization often did not take place in isolation, but in groups, for example through circles of friends, in which the ideology of IS gradually spread.

THE IDEOLOGY OF THE CALIPHATE: SHARIA, GOVERNANCE AND THE UMMAH

The ideology of the caliphate is a complex and deep-rooted religious-political doctrine in Islam that revolves around the concepts of Sharia (Islamic law), governance (rule), and the umma (the Islamic community). This ideology has taken on various forms over the centuries, and its understanding is of great importance in the modern world for both Muslim communities and non-Muslim actors.

The caliphate, which refers to the Arabic word "chalīfa", literally means "successor" or "deputy". Historically, it refers to the succession of the Prophet Muhammad after his death in 632 AD. The first caliph, Abu Bakr, was elected as Muhammad's successor to lead the Muslim community. The caliphate developed into a central institution in Islamic history, embodying both religious and political authority.

The classical caliphate included the first four "rightly guided caliphs" (al-khulafā' al-rāshidūn), who represented the ideal of just Islamic rule. These caliphs, Abu Bakr, Umar, Uthman and Ali, were considered role models for Islamic leadership and set standards for governance according to Islamic principles.

Sharia, Islamic law, is the backbone of the ideology of the caliphate. It is based on the Koran, the hadiths (traditions of the Prophet) and the Sunni legal tradition. Sharia regulates all aspects of a Muslim's life, from religious practices to social and economic relations to political governance.

In the context of the caliphate, Sharia law is considered the basis of rule. The caliph's job is to implement Sharia law and ensure that society lives according to the divine commandments. This means that governance in the caliphate is not only a political responsibility, but also a religious one. The caliph is the one who enforces Sharia law in the ummah and thus ensures order and justice according to Islamic principles.

The implementation of Sharia as state law in the caliphate differs from modern secular legal systems because it does not recognize a separation between religion and state. Governance in the caliphate is theocratic, with political decisions derived directly from religious principles.

The Ummah, the community of believers, is a central concept in the ideology of the caliphate. It includes all Muslims worldwide and forms a supranational community united by faith in Islam. The Caliphate sees itself as the political institution that is supposed to ensure the unity of the Ummah.

In the ideology of the Caliphate, the Ummah is the foundation of Islamic society, united by common religious beliefs and practices. The Caliph is the leader of this community and is responsible for the well-being of all Muslims. This transnational perspective contrasts with modern nation-states, which are based on territorial borders and ethnic identity.

In the caliphate, the ummah is regarded as an entity that transcends cultural, ethnic and linguistic differences. This notion is particularly important in times of divisions within the Muslim world, as it promotes the idea of a common Islamic identity. Historically, the caliphate has often been a symbol of the unity of the Muslim world, even if this unity has often been difficult to achieve in practice.

The ideology of the Caliphate has undergone different interpretations over time, especially in the context of the modern world. While the classical caliphate originated in the 7th century, the concept has been revived in modern times by various Islamist movements calling for the reintroduction of a caliphate based on Sharia principles.

Modern movements such as Salafism and political Islam see the caliphate as an ideal state in which Islamic rule is to be restored. These movements argue that the renunciation of Sharia law and the dissolution of the Caliphate in the 20th century (through the abolition of the Ottoman Caliphate in 1924) plunged the Muslim world into a crisis that can only be overcome by returning to the Caliphate.

At the same time, the ideology of the caliphate faces significant challenges in the modern world. The idea of a transnational Islamic government is at odds with the existing political structures of the nation-states. In addition, the implementation of Sharia law is often seen as incompatible with human rights and democratic principles, which leads to considerable tensions.

THE CONCEPT OF THE CALIPHATE IN THE 21ST CENTURY: THEORY AND PRACTICE

The caliphate, one of the most influential political and religious institutions in the history of Islam, has undergone numerous transformations since its founding in the 7th century. Originally established as a successor institution to the Prophet Muhammad (570-632 AD), the caliphate symbolized the unity of the Muslim community (ummah) and the union of religious and secular power. In the 21st century, however, the caliphate has taken on a new and often controversial meaning, especially in the context of global terrorism and political Islamism.

Historical development of the caliphate
After the death of the Prophet Muhammad in 632 AD, the caliphate emerged as the institutional solution to the question of succession. The first four caliphs, known as the Rashidun caliphs (632-661 AD), ruled a rapidly expanding Muslim community that had to be led both religiously and politically. This early period of the Caliphate was considered the "golden age" in which the caliphs were both moral and administrative role models.

The subsequent Umayyad dynasty (661-750 AD) fundamentally changed the caliphate. They moved the seat of the caliphate from Medina to Damascus, transforming the originally rather egalitarian Islamic community into a powerful empire that stretched across large parts of the Middle East, North Africa and Spain. Under the Umayyads, the caliphate increasingly developed into a monarchical institution relying on an aristocratic elite, which led to internal tensions and uprisings, especially among the Shiites.

The Abbasids (750-1258 AD) took over the caliphate after the fall of the Umayyads and moved the capital to Baghdad. Under her rule, Islamic civilization experienced a cultural and scientific heyday. The Caliphate became more centralized under the Abbasids and developed a more extensive bureaucracy. During this time, the foundations of Islamic law (Sharia) were codified and the caliphate as an institution was firmly embedded in the religious and political culture of Islam.

However, the Caliphate also began to lose its power during the Abbasid period, as it was increasingly challenged by regional dynasties that established de facto independent rulers. This weakening continued until the Abbasid Caliphate finally came to an end in 1258 due to the Mongol invasion of Baghdad, although the Caliphate in Egypt was symbolically continued under the rule of the Mamluks (1261-1517).

The caliphate experienced a revival under the Ottomans, who claimed it in 1517 after the conquest of Egypt. Under Ottoman rule, the caliphate became a symbol of Islamic unity, while the sultan acted primarily as a secular ruler. This form of caliphate was heavily influenced by the realities of the Ottoman state structure and the geopolitical challenges the empire had to overcome throughout its long history.

The end of the Ottoman Caliphate in 1924 by Mustafa Kemal Ataturk marked a turning point in the history of the Muslim world. The loss of the caliphate led to a deep identity crisis among Muslims and sparked debates about how Islam and its political structures should be redefined in the modern world.

Theoretical foundations of the caliphate
In classical Islamic thought, the caliphate plays a central role. For scholars such as Al-Mawardi (972-1058) and Ibn Khaldun (1332-1406), the caliphate was not only a political institution, but also a religious duty to ensure the well-being of the Ummah. Al-Mawardi emphasized that the caliph, as the successor of the Prophet, should direct both the secular and religious affairs of the Muslim community. He developed detailed criteria for the election and removal of a caliph and considered the caliphate necessary to uphold Sharia law and ensure the unity of the ummah.

Ibn Khaldun, on the other hand, viewed the caliphate from a more sociological perspective. In his work "Muqaddima", he analysed the cyclical nature of political power in the Muslim world and argued that the caliphate could only be stable and legitimate if it was based on a strong social fabric, which he referred to as "asabiyya".

In the 20th century, the abolition of the Caliphate and the colonization of the Muslim world led to a new wave of Islamic thought. Islamic scholars and activists such as Hassan al-Banna (1906-1949) and Sayyid Qutb (1906-1966) saw the caliphate as a lost but essential institution that needed to be restored to rid the Muslim world of Western imperialism and internal corruption. Qutb, a pioneer of the Muslim Brotherhood, saw the caliphate as a necessary step towards the establishment of an Islamic state that would be governed strictly according to Sharia law. For him, the caliphate was the ultimate form of political and religious authority, superior to the modern, secular order.

On the other hand, reformist thinkers such as Ali Abdel Raziq (1888-1966) argued that the caliphate was not necessary, and that Islam did not prescribe a specific political order. In his work "Islam and the Foundations of Rule" (1925), Raziq argued that the caliphate was a historical institution that could not be derived from the Koran or the Sunnah. He called on Muslims to adopt modern, democratic systems that are better suited to the challenges of the present.

During the 20th and 21st centuries, different currents have developed in Islam, which interpret the caliphate differently. While traditional Salafists view the caliphate as a return to the "pure" Islamic practice of the early days, many modern Muslims reject the idea of a centralized caliphate in favor of a pluralistic, nation-state order. These tensions reflect the broader debate within the Muslim world about how to deal with tradition and modernity.

Practice of the Caliphate in the 21st Century

The most radical manifestation of the caliphate in the 21st century was the proclamation of the caliphate by the Islamic State (IS) in 2014. Under the leadership of Abu Bakr al-Baghdadi, IS declared a caliphate that would unite the entire Muslim world and rule according to a strict interpretation of Sharia law. ISIS's ideology is based on an extremist interpretation of Salafism and jihadism, which sees violence as a legitimate means of realizing a "pure" Islamic state.

In practice, however, ISIS's "caliphate" was characterized by brutal human rights violations, systematic terror, and a rigid, often distorted interpretation of Islamic law. ISIS's territorial expansion in parts of Syria and Iraq has led to unprecedented levels of destruction and displacement. Although ISIS has been largely defeated militarily, its ideology remains a threatening legacy that continues to mobilize followers worldwide.

The proclamation of the caliphate by IS triggered shock waves worldwide. In the Muslim world, ISIS has been widely opposed, especially by leading Islamic scholars and institutions such as Al-Azhar University in Egypt. They emphasized that the caliphate of the IS is neither religiously legitimate nor historically authentic. Many Muslims viewed ISIS as a threat to both Islam and international security.

At the same time, the IS caliphate led to the radicalization of some Muslim communities, especially in Europe, where young Muslims who felt marginalized and alienated were attracted by ISIS propaganda. These developments have caused deep social divisions and intensified the debate about integration, radicalization and the place of Islam in Western societies.

The establishment of the IS caliphate had significant geopolitical implications. Instability in the Middle East, especially in Syria and Iraq, intensified as ISIS conquered large areas and established a "state" within those borders. The international community, led by the United States and a coalition of Western and regional allies, launched a military campaign to defeat ISIS. This intervention led to the widespread destruction of ISIS's territorial base, but the group remains active, particularly through asymmetric warfare and terrorist attacks.

The fight against ISIS has also altered the regional balance of power in the Middle East, with countries such as Iran, Turkey and Russia playing a significant role in the post-war orders of Syria and Iraq. At the same time, the fight against IS has led to increased militarization and authoritarian tendencies in many affected states, which could have long-term effects on the political development of the region.

Prospects of the caliphate in the 21st century
Even after the collapse of the IS caliphate, the idea of the caliphate remains an ideological challenge that continues to be

propagated by various Islamist groups and individuals. The continuing attractiveness of the caliphate, especially among young people who feel alienated in their societies, requires new approaches to prevention work and political education. It is necessary to understand and combat the causes of radicalisation to prevent the resurgence of extremist ideologies.

In a globalized world, the concept of the caliphate also raises questions about the role of Islam in the international system. Some thinkers argue for a redefinition of the caliphate that focuses more on ethical and spiritual leadership rather than territorial and political claims. Such approaches could build a bridge between traditional Islamic political theory and modern requirements for governance and international cooperation.

One possible path for the future of the caliphate could be through a pluralistic approach that recognizes diversity within the Islamic world and allows for the political expression of Islam in different contexts. This could result in the promotion of democratic processes and human rights within Muslim societies without compromising the religious foundations of Islam. The challenge is to develop a model that both does justice to the historical roots of the caliphate and meets the modern needs of Muslim communities worldwide.

The concept of the caliphate in the 21st century stands in the field of tension between tradition and modernity, between religious symbolism and political reality. While the historical caliphate was a complex institution that fulfilled both religious and political functions, modern interpretations, especially by extremist groups such as ISIS, have made the caliphate a symbol of resistance to the West and a return to a supposedly "pure" Islamic order.

Nevertheless, for many Muslims, the caliphate remains an important theological concept that is deeply rooted in the history and identity of Islam. The challenge for the Muslim world in the 21st century is to reinterpret the Caliphate in a way that meets the demands and values of the modern world without undermining its religious and historical significance. The future of the caliphate will therefore depend heavily on how Muslim communities around the world respond to the tensions between tradition and modernity and how they can shape a harmonious integration of religion and politics in a globalized world.

IS AND ITS INFLUENCE ON ISLAMIC COMMUNITIES WORLDWIDE

The Islamic State gained international attention in 2014 when it proclaimed a caliphate and took control of large parts of Iraq and Syria. The organization, which is characterized by extreme violence and a radical interpretation of Islam, has had a profound impact on Islamic communities worldwide.

ISIS is ideologically based on an extremist interpretation of Salafism, a conservative current in Islam that seeks a return to the practices of the "pious ancestors" (al-salaf al-salih). While Salafism in its original form aims at strict adherence to the Koran and the Sunnah, IS combines this doctrine with a militant form of jihadism. This ideology justifies the use of force to establish a "pure" Islamic state, governed according to Sharia principles.

ISIS ideologues, including Abu Bakr al-Baghdadi and Abu Muhammad al-Adnani, developed a theology that promotes global jihad and calls on all Muslims to support or participate in this struggle. ISIS declared the restoration of the caliphate to be a divine mandate and presented itself as the only legitimate authority for Muslims worldwide.

A central component of ISIS ideology is takfirism, a practice in which Muslims who do not follow the extremist interpretation of Islam are considered apostates (kuffar). ISIS rigorously applies this practice by declaring both Shiites and Sunnis who oppose its ideology to be enemies. This exclusivity and claim to the absolute truth have enabled ISIS to promote an extremist identity that leaves little room for dialogue or compromise.

ISIS's takfirism has not only led to massive intra-Islamic conflicts, but also to the legitimation of violence against Muslim communities that deviate from ISIS ideology. This has led to a deep division within Islam worldwide and further destabilized the already fragile balance between different Islamic currents.

One of the most serious effects of IS on Islamic communities worldwide is the radicalization and recruitment of followers. ISIS cleverly used social media and other digital platforms to spread its ideology and recruit followers. Young Muslims in Western countries who felt marginalized or alienated were targeted by IS propaganda. IS presented itself as an alternative to Western societies, which were perceived as corrupt, and promised recruits a clear identity and a purpose in the "holy war".

Thousands of young men and women from Europe, North America, North Africa and Central Asia traveled to ISIS-controlled areas to join the group. This transnational mobilization led to a global security crisis, as many of the recruits returned to their countries of origin after the defeat of ISIS, often more radicalized than before.

The returnees posed a significant threat to national security and forced governments around the world to rethink their counterterrorism strategies. In addition, ISIS's recruitment campaign led to further stigmatization of Muslim communities in Western countries that were already struggling with Islamophobia and social exclusion.

IS has had a profound influence on Muslim communities around the world not only in terms of security policy, but also in terms of social and cultural policy. In countries with significant Muslim populations, especially in Europe, the emergence of ISIS led to increased Islamophobia and growing distrust of Muslims. The association of Islam with terrorism, promoted by ISIS propaganda, had serious consequences for the integration of Muslim communities and the perception of Islam in the Western world.

This negative perception led to an exacerbation of tensions between Muslim communities and the majority society. Many Muslims have been forced to publicly distance themselves from the atrocities committed by ISIS while defending their own religious identity. This created a dilemma, as the need to separate Islam from extremist interpretations collided with the pressure not to delegitimize their own religious community.

In some cases, this led to a stronger identification with Islam and a return to religious values to counteract the IS discourse.

In other cases, however, the ongoing stigma and discrimination led to further alienation and occasionally radicalisation.

ISIS's influence also extended to international politics and relations between states. ISIS served as a catalyst for geopolitical conflicts, especially in the Middle East, where various states became involved in the conflict, whether through direct military interventions or by supporting rival groups. The rise of ISIS exacerbated existing tensions between Sunni and Shiite states and intensified competition for influence in the region, especially between Saudi Arabia and Iran.

The threat of ISIS also led to new alliances and cooperation, especially within the framework of the international coalition against ISIS, led by the United States. At the same time, the conflicts fueled by IS have led to massive refugee movements, which has triggered a crisis in Europe that has further increased political and social tensions.

In countries such as Iraq and Syria, IS left a trail of destruction in its wake, which led to a deep political, social and economic crisis. Rebuilding these societies and healing the wounds caused by IS will take decades and will require extensive international cooperation and targeted support for the affected communities.

Islamic scholars and institutions around the world have resolutely opposed the ideology of IS. Leading Islamic authorities, such as Al-Azhar University in Egypt, the highest authority on

Sunni Islam, have issued fatwas against ISIS and its practices. These religious declarations emphasized that ISIS's teachings are incompatible with the fundamental principles of Islam and that ISIS promotes a distorted and dangerous interpretation of religion.

Many Muslim scholars have worked hard to question the legitimacy of the IS caliphate and refute its theological foundations. They argued that ISIS's caliphate was both religiously and historically illegitimate, and that there was no basis for the extreme violence that ISIS exercised in the name of Islam. These efforts are aimed at informing and educating Muslims worldwide to prevent them from being influenced by ISIS's radical ideology.

In addition to religious responses, Muslim communities around the world have also launched grassroots initiatives to counter radicalization. These initiatives range from educational programs designed to help young Muslims develop a sound and nuanced understanding of their religion to deradicalization programs aimed at reaching those who have already been radicalized.

One example of such an initiative is the Strong Cities Network, which connects cities around the world to share best practices on preventing extremism. Such programs place a strong emphasis on directly involving communities to consider local contexts and develop preventive measures tailored to the specific needs and challenges on the ground.

In addition, numerous Muslim organizations in Europe and North America have launched projects that are intended to promote integration and at the same time strengthen Islamic identity in a pluralistic context. These projects often emphasize the values of peace, justice, and community, and seek to promote a positive and authentic Muslim identity that opposes ISIS's extremist narratives.

In some countries, the influence of ISIS has also led to increased political mobilization of Muslim communities. In the face of increasing Islamophobia and the threat of extremism, many Muslims have become politically engaged to defend their rights and actively participate in shaping society. This has led to a greater presence of Muslims in political movements and parties, and in some cases to increased participation in electoral processes.

However, this mobilization has also brought challenges, as Muslim activists often face mistrust and prejudice. Nevertheless, political participation is an important aspect of the response to ISIS, as it gives Muslim communities the opportunity to articulate their concerns and actively contribute to the promotion of peace and security.

ISIS has exerted an unprecedented influence on Islamic communities worldwide, leaving deep scars on the global Islamic landscape. While ISIS's ideology appeals only to a minority within Islam, the group has nevertheless caused significant social, cultural and political upheaval. Muslim communities have responded to ISIS's challenge with a mix of religious activism, grassroots movements, and political mobilization.

The continuing threat of extremist ideologies, such as ISIS, requires a continued effort to promote dialogue and understanding within the Muslim world and to strengthen the forces working for peace, justice and a pluralistic future. The lessons of ISIS's influence will also be central to the future shaping of relations between Islam and the global community. It remains crucial that Muslims around the world raise their voices to fight against extremism and defend the true values of their religion.

THE ROLE OF IS IN THE SYRIAN CIVIL WAR

The Islamic State played a central but complex and destructive role in the Syrian civil war, one of the bloodiest and longest-running conflicts of the 21st century. Since its appearance on the Syrian stage, ISIS has not only changed the dynamics of the civil war, but also introduced a new dimension of violence and international engagement into the conflict.

From the outset, ISIS's military strategy in Syria has been aggressive and focused on territorial expansion. The group captured key cities and regions, including Raqqa, which became its unofficial capital, as well as large parts of the eastern provinces of Deir ez-Zor and Hasakah. ISIS used a mixture of military strength, brutal tactics and ideological propaganda to both terrorize its opponents and control local communities.

ISIS differed from other actors in the Syrian civil war by its ability to effectively manage conquered territories. The group established a network of local administrative units, which were governed according to the strict interpretations of Sharia. These administrative structures included courts, police and social services, all of which were under the direct control of the IS leadership. This allowed IS not only to exercise military control, but also to ideologically indoctrinate the population and exploit it economically.

The brutality of IS was a central aspect of his strategy. Public executions, beheadings, enslavements, and other forms of extreme violence were used to terrorize both local populations and international adversaries. These tactics were aimed at breaking resistance and consolidating control over the conquered territories. ISIS's use of social media to propagate this violence gave the group an additional global reach and increased fear of it worldwide.

In June 2014, IS proclaimed the caliphate, with Raqqa as its capital. This step was not only symbolically significant, but also showed ISIS's ambitions to establish lasting Islamic rule. Raqqa became a center of ISIS's power, from which the group coordinated its military operations and ideological propaganda campaigns.

The rise of ISIS has had a profound impact on the course of the Syrian civil war and the dynamics of the conflict. Through its military successes and control over large parts of Syria, IS changed the balance of power in the country and posed new challenges to both the Syrian government and other rebel groups.

IS contributed significantly to the intensification of violence in the Syrian civil war. The brutality of his tactics and his aggressive expansionist efforts led to a further fragmentation of the opposition. Many rebel groups that originally fought against the Assad regime were forced to direct their resources against ISIS, weakening the opposition's ability to fight the regime.

In addition, the presence of ISIS led to new front lines and conflicts between different armed groups. This fragmentation of the opposition made it more difficult to develop a coordinated strategy against the Assad regime and led to a longer and more complex conflict.

From 2016, IS began to lose ground militarily in Syria. The combined offensive by Syrian government forces, Kurdish militias and international coalition forces led to significant losses for IS. In 2017, Raqqa was recaptured after months of fighting, and ISIS gradually lost control of its most important territories.

Despite these military defeats, ISIS retreated to rural areas and desert regions and changed its tactics to guerrilla warfare and terrorist attacks. This adaptation of ISIS meant that while the group was no longer able to control large areas, it continued to pose a threat of asymmetric warfare.

IS left behind a deeply divided and destroyed society in Syria. The destruction of infrastructure, the mass displacement of people and the ongoing insecurity hampered efforts to rebuild and stabilize. In addition, the ideology of ISIS remains present in parts of the population, which poses the risk of renewed radicalization and the resurgence of extremist movements.

THE EXPANSION OF IS: FROM NORTH AFRICA TO SOUTHEAST ASIA

ISIS began as a regional terrorist group in Iraq and Syria, but quickly developed into a global threat. Through its aggressive expansion and clever propaganda, ISIS has been able to gain supporters and offshoots in many parts of the world in a relatively short time, especially in North Africa and Southeast Asia. This expansion, characterized by a combination of ideological proliferation, direct military intervention, and the creation of franchises, had profound implications for regional stability and international security.

ISIS's expansion was based on a radical extremist ideology based on the idea of a global caliphate. This ideology called for the creation of an Islamic state that would extend across national borders. Unlike al-Qaeda, which operated in a more decentralized manner, IS pursued a strategy of territorial control and direct government over the conquered territories.

Libya played a central role in ISIS's expansion in North Africa. After the overthrow of Muammar Gaddafi in 2011, Libya descended into chaos, with rival militias fighting for control. In this power vacuum, IS saw an opportunity to expand its presence. In 2014, IS captured the coastal city of Sirte, which became the group's stronghold and unofficial capital in North Africa.

In Sirte, IS established a government structure like that in Syria and Iraq, introduced Sharia law and established a local administration. The city became an important recruitment and training center for jihadists from all over the region. ISIS also used Libya as a base for attacks on neighboring countries and sought to extend its control to other parts of the country, including Benghazi and Derna.

Another important arena of ISIS's expansion in North Africa was the Sinai Peninsula in Egypt. The local jihadist group Ansar Bait al-Maqdis swore allegiance to ISIS in 2014 and renamed itself Wilayat Sinai, which means "Sinai Province". This group carried out a series of terrorist attacks targeting both Egyptian security forces and international targets, such as the downing of the Russian passenger plane Kogalymavia Flight 9268 in October 2015.

The presence of ISIS in the Sinai Peninsula posed a significant challenge for the Egyptian government, which had difficulty controlling the confusing and hard-to-reach region. ISIS took advantage of the region's isolation and poverty to recruit local communities and continue its activities.

IS also tried to gain a foothold in Algeria and Tunisia. In Algeria, some radical groups previously linked to Al-Qaeda swore allegiance to ISIS and carried out attacks under its banner. In Tunisia, which faced significant political and social tensions following the 2011 revolution, ISIS carried out several high-profile attacks, including the attack on the Bardo Museum in Tunis and the massacre of tourists in Sousse in 2015. These
80

attacks had a far-reaching impact on the Tunisian economy, especially the tourism sector, and increased security concerns throughout the region.

In Southeast Asia, ISIS became particularly active in the Philippines, where it established links with local jihadist groups such as Abu Sayyaf and Maute. Abu Sayyaf, a group originally known for its kidnappings and ransoms, swore allegiance to ISIS in 2014. The group changed its tactics and goals to be more in line with ISIS's global ambitions.

The peak of ISIS activity in the Philippines was the siege of the city of Marawi in May 2017, when fighters from the Maute group, backed by Abu Sayyaf, took control of the city and held it against Philippine forces for several months. The siege led to intense fighting in which the city was largely destroyed and hundreds of thousands of people were displaced. Marawi became a symbol of ISIS's ability to gain territorial influence in Southeast Asia and globalize local conflicts.

IS also tried to gain a foothold in Indonesia and Malaysia, two of the world's most populous Muslim countries. In Indonesia, which has a long history of jihadist movements, ISIS used existing networks to spread its ideology and carry out attacks. The Indonesian group Jemaah Ansharut Daulah (JAD) pledged allegiance to ISIS and carried out a series of terrorist attacks, including the attack on the center of Jakarta in January 2016.

In Malaysia, ISIS also tried to gain followers and plan attacks, although the Malaysian government took extensive security measures to prevent this. Despite the strict surveillance, IS was able to recruit some followers in Malaysia and carry out smaller attacks.

One of the main methods used by ISIS in its expansion was ideological recruitment. The group used existing local conflicts, political instability and socio-economic discontent to spread its message and recruit followers. The promise of a caliphate in which injustices are eliminated and a "pure" Islam is practiced attracted many marginalized and radicalized individuals.

IS was also able to use local conflicts for its own purposes. In North Africa, he took advantage of the chaos in Libya, while in Southeast Asia he benefited from the long-standing separatist movements in the Philippines. This ability to connect local issues to its global ideology was critical to the group's success in expanding.

ISIS used targeted military tactics to promote its expansion. This included both conventional military operations, such as the siege of cities, and unconventional tactics, such as guerrilla warfare and terrorist attacks. In many cases, ISIS aimed at conquering and controlling territories where it could enforce its strict interpretations of Sharia law.

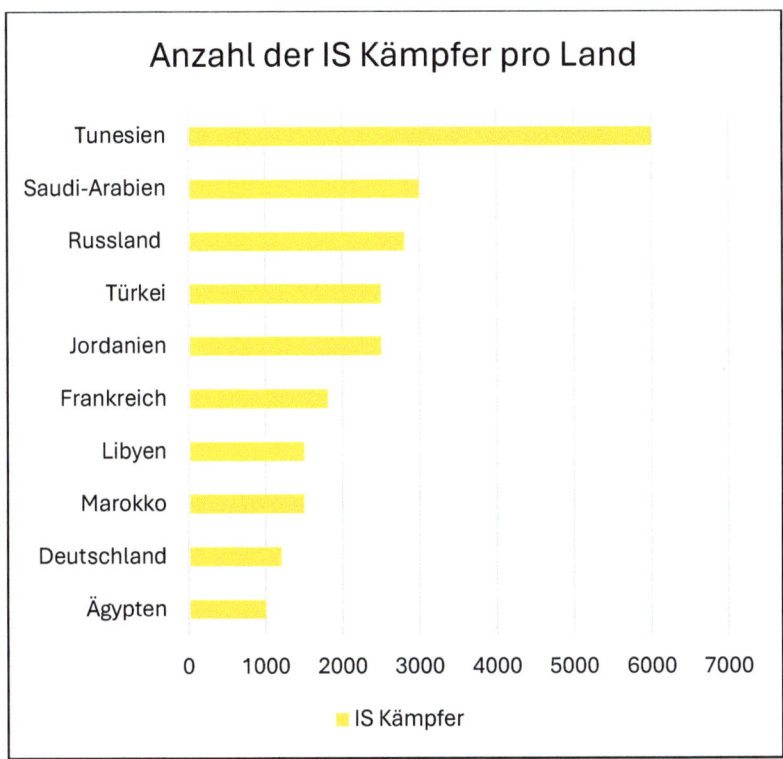

Anzahl der IS Kämpfer pro Land

The graph shows the number of ISIS fighters per country, indicating the prevalence and recruitment of extremists in different regions. Tunisia tops the list with 6,000 fighters, followed by Saudi Arabia (3,000) and Russia (2,800).

These figures shed light on the geographical and social factors that lead to the recruitment of young men in these countries.

Tunisia can serve as an example of the post-Arab Spring challenges, where social unrest and economic difficulties provide a breeding ground for extremism.

Saudi Arabia has been criticized for its religious policies, which may contribute to radicalization, while **Russia** struggles with its ethnic diversity and geopolitical conflicts that can promote radicalization.

The number of IS fighters from **Jordan, Turkey, France, Libya, Morocco** and **Germany** makes it clear that IS also has an appeal in Western and North African countries.

PARTNER ORGANIZATION OF THE ISLAMIC STATE

The Islamic State (IS) has cooperated with various organizations and groups, which often pursue similar ideological goals or have entered alliances for strategic reasons. These groups have played various roles, ranging from direct support to the creation of offshoots of ISIS.

Boko Haram (Nigeria) swore allegiance to IS in March 2015 and became the "West Africa Province" (Wilayat Gharb Ifriqiyyah) of IS. The group carried out terrorist operations in Nigeria and neighboring countries, adopting the ideology and tactics of ISIS. Boko Haram played a key role in the spread of ISIS ideology in West Africa.

Abu Sayyaf (Philippines) This militant group in the Philippines has also sworn allegiance to ISIS and operates under the name ISIS East Asian Province. Abu Sayyaf has supported IS through kidnappings, ransom extortion and military actions in

Southeast Asia. They contributed to the spread of IS ideology in the region.

Ansar Bait al-Maqdis (Egypt/Sinai) This group swore allegiance to ISIS in November 2014 and became ISIS's "Sinai Province". It carried out numerous attacks on Egyptian security forces and tourists in Sinai. The group played an important role in strengthening ISIS's presence in Egypt and North Africa.

Jund al-Khilafah (Algeria) This Algerian group joined ISIS in 2014 and operates under the name "Soldiers of the Caliphate". It carried out attacks in Algeria, including the kidnapping and murder of a French tourist. Their role was to strengthen IS in North Africa.

ISIS in the Caucasus (Russia) Militants from the North Caucasus, especially from Chechnya and Dagestan, have sworn allegiance to ISIS and established their own "Caucasus Province". This group carried out attacks in Russia and recruited fighters for ISIS in Syria and Iraq. It played an important role in the international recruitment of fighters.

Taliban factions (Afghanistan/Pakistan) Some Taliban factions have joined or cooperated with ISIS, especially in the Khorasan region (Afghanistan/Pakistan), known as the Islamic State of Khorasan (IS-K). This group carried out attacks against the Afghan government and the Taliban and promoted the spread of ISIS in Central Asia.

Libyan militias (Libya) Various militias in Libya, including former supporters of Muammar al-Gaddafi, have joined ISIS or cooperated to gain control of areas. IS Libya being at times one of the strongest foreign offshoots of IS and at times-controlled cities such as Sirte.

Ahrar al-Sham (Syria) During the Syrian civil war, there were phases of cooperation between ISIS and other Islamist groups, especially in the initial phase of the conflict. This cooperation often served tactical goals, such as joint operations against the Syrian government or rival rebel groups.

Islamic State in the Greater Sahara Province (ISGS) This group operates in the Sahel, particularly in Mali, Niger and Burkina Faso. ISGS was created in 2015 and declared its allegiance to ISIS in 2016. It carries out attacks on local security forces and international troops and plays a central role in spreading ISIS's influence in the Sahel region.

Islamic State in Yemen This group emerged as an offshoot of IS in 2014 and carried out numerous attacks against the Shiite Houthi rebels and the Yemeni government. It competes with al-Qaeda in the Arabian Peninsula (AQAP) for supremacy in Yemen but supports ISIS's overarching goal of establishing a global caliphate state.

Islamic State in Somalia This group was formed in 2015 as a spin-off from al-Shabaab, a group linked to al-Qaeda. IS in Somalia focuses on recruiting and carrying out attacks in Somalia and East Africa. Its role is to establish and strengthen ISIS's presence in the region.

Caucasus Emirate (Emarat Kavkaz) Although the Caucasus Emirate has traditionally been linked to al-Qaeda, some splinter groups have sworn allegiance to ISIS and operate in

Russia's North Caucasus regions. These groups carry out attacks on Russian security forces and recruit fighters for IS.

Islamic Movement of Uzbekistan (IMU) The IMU was originally linked to the Taliban and al-Qaeda, but in 2015 a faction of the IMU swore allegiance to ISIS. This group operates in Central Asia, particularly in Afghanistan, Uzbekistan and Tajikistan, and supports ISIS through recruitment and military operations.

Wilayat al Sudan al Gharbi (West Africa, excluding Nigeria) This group, which is active in various West African countries such as Niger, Chad and Cameroon, has joined ISIS and operates in a similar way to Boko Haram. It carries out attacks on civilian and military targets and spreads the IS ideology in West Africa.

Khorasan group in Bangladesh This group was formed in Bangladesh and swore allegiance to IS. She carried out several attacks on local and international targets, including the 2016 attack on the Holey Artisan Bakery in Dhaka. The group serves as the local arm of IS in South Asia.

Mujahideen Shura Council (Gaza) A group of Salafists in Gaza that has sworn allegiance to ISIS and occasionally carries out rocket attacks on Israel. This group promotes ISIS ideology in the Palestinian territories but is small in the region.

Maute Group (Philippines) This group was instrumental in the attempt to bring the city of Marawi in the Philippines under IS control in 2017. The Maute Group has sworn allegiance to ISIS and has played a key role in expanding ISIS's presence in Southeast Asia.

Jamaat Ansar al-Sharia (Libya) Although this group was originally independent, there were phases of cooperation with IS in Libya, especially in the context of the civil war. They supported IS in controlling areas in Libya and coordinated military actions.

Wilayat Khurasan in India This group is responsible for recruiting and carrying out attacks in India and represents ISIS in South Asia. Their activities include propaganda and the promotion of attacks in India.

Al-Mourabitoun (Mali) This group was originally an independent jihadist organization that operated under Mokhtar Belmokhtar. While some of their factions have remained loyal to al-Qaeda, others have pledged allegiance to ISIS and support its operations in Mali and the Sahara.

Wilayat al-Haramayn (Saudi Arabia) This cell operates in Saudi Arabia and has declared war on the country's government. It carried out several attacks on Shiite mosques and security forces. The group aims to gain control of the holy cities of Mecca and Medina and spread ISIS ideology in the Arabian Peninsula.

Islamic State in Kashmir This group operates in the disputed region of Kashmir and is trying to expand the IS presence in South Asia. It carried out attacks on Indian security forces and recruits local fighters for the IS cause.

Islamic State in Congo (ISCAP) This group, officially known as the Islamic State in Central Africa, is active in the Democratic Republic of Congo and Mozambique. It is committing acts of violence against civilians and government forces and is trying to strengthen the IS presence in the Central African region.

Islamic State in Mozambique (Al-Shabaab Mozambique) This group is active in Mozambique and has a strong presence in the province of Cabo Delgado. It carries out brutal attacks on villages and security forces and tries to establish a province under IS control in Mozambique.

Islamic State in Tunisia This group is active in Tunisia and has carried out several attacks, including the attack on the Bardo Museum and Sousse beach. It recruits local fighters and supports the IS agenda in North Africa.

Wilayat Khurasan in Pakistan This group operates in Pakistan and Afghanistan, especially in the Khyber Pakhtunkhwa region. It carries out attacks against the Pakistani government and Shiite communities to strengthen the IS presence in South Asia.

Wilayat Algeria This group operates in Algeria and originated from the Algerian branch of al-Qaeda. It carried out attacks on security forces and tourists and tried to spread the IS ideology in North Africa.

Islamic State in Yemen (Wilayat al-Yaman) This group is one of the smaller IS organizations and carries out sporadic attacks in Yemen. It competes with al-Qaeda in the Arabian Peninsula (AQAP) for supremacy in the region.

Islamic State in the Caucasus region (IS-Caucasus) This group recruits fighters from Russia's North Caucasus, especially from Chechnya and Dagestan. It supports IS by attacking Russian security forces and promotes IS ideology in the region.

Wilayat Turkiya (Turkey) This cell is active in Turkey and carried out attacks against the Turkish government and tourists. The group also uses Turkey as a transit country for fighters traveling to Syria and Iraq.

Wilayat al-Furat (Syria/Iraq) This region stretches across the Euphrates and includes areas in Syria and Iraq. The group operated mainly in the areas controlled by ISIS and coordinated military operations along the river.

Ansar al-Sharia in Tunisia This group was originally considered part of the global jihadist network and operated independently before pledging allegiance to ISIS. It has been involved in several attacks in Tunisia and promotes IS ideology in North Africa.

Wilayat Jazeera (Syria/Iraq) This region includes parts of Syria and Iraq and has been a key region for the logistics and transfer of fighters. It served as a strategic hub for IS operations in the Middle East.

Wilayat Hauran (southern Syria) This group operated in the Hauran region in southern Syria and carried out attacks against the Syrian government and rival rebels. The group contributed to the territorial expansion of IS in Syria.

IS partner organizations locations

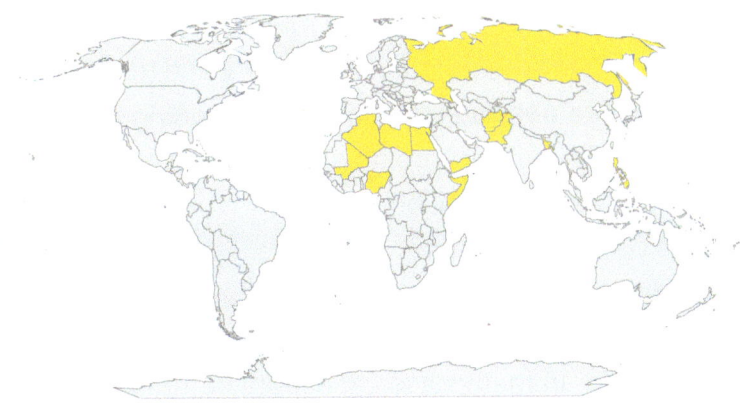

THE ROLE OF THE DIASPORA IN THE SUPPORT FOR IS

The role of diaspora communities in supporting political movements and conflicts in their home countries is a multi-layered and complex phenomenon. In the case of the Islamic State, parts of the Muslim diaspora in various countries have played a role in supporting the organization. This support manifested itself in the form of financial contributions, recruitment, propaganda and even the travel of people to the areas controlled by ISIS.

The term "diaspora" refers to communities that live outside their country of origin, often because of migration, flight or displacement. These communities often maintain strong cultural, religious, and social ties to their home country and play an important role in maintaining identity and traditions. However, diaspora communities are also actors in transnational networks that maintain political, economic and social connections across national borders.

Diaspora communities have the potential to play both positive and negative roles in the political developments of their countries of origin. In many cases, diaspora communities support political or militant movements in their home country through financial contributions, lobbying, or by promoting ideological narratives. This support can be based on both positive motivations, such as the promotion of democracy and human rights, and negative motivations, such as ethnic nationalism or religious extremism.

In the case of ISIS, part of the Muslim diaspora has used these transnational networks to further the goals of the extremist organization. This support often came through informal channels and networks that are difficult to monitor and regulate.

One of the most important forms of diaspora support for ISIS has been financial. ISIS used various ways to raise funds from followers in the diaspora, including appeals for donations on social media, using charities as a cover, and by transferring funds directly. This financial support was used to finance military operations, to supply the fighters and to maintain control over the occupied territories.

Some members of the diaspora felt motivated by religious or ideological beliefs to support IS financially. Others may have been forced to donate money due to family ties or social pressures. The use of cryptocurrencies and other anonymous payment methods also made it difficult for security agencies to track and stop these transactions.

Another significant aspect of diaspora support was the recruitment of fighters and followers. IS operated a sophisticated propaganda machine that works primarily through social media and online platforms. This propaganda was specifically aimed at young Muslims in the diaspora who felt marginalized or alienated in their host countries.

Recruitment was often done through personal networks based on trust and shared religious or ideological beliefs. Members of the diaspora who had fought in ISIS areas played an important role in recruitment, serving as role models and portraying life in the "caliphate" as desirable. Some diaspora communities have faced a wave of exodus, with young men and women leaving their families and countries to join ISIS.

The role of the diaspora in the ideological support of IS should not be underestimated. Diaspora members, who had a high level of education and access to media platforms, played a crucial role in spreading ISIS ideology. This support manifested itself in the production of online content that spread ISIS's ideology, including videos, blogs, and social media posts.

The spread of this propaganda helped ISIS reach a global audience and spread its ideology far beyond the borders of the Middle East. Especially in Western countries, this form of support helped to radicalize the discourse on Islam and exacerbate tensions between Muslim communities and mainstream society.

A main motive for diaspora members' support for ISIS was ideological conviction. Some Muslims in the diaspora were attracted to the idea of an "Islamic state" governed according to Sharia principles. The promise of a return to a "pure" form of Islam and the opportunity to participate in the creation of a new Islamic polity offered a powerful vision for some.

This ideological appeal was reinforced by ISIS's propaganda, which portrayed the conflict as part of a larger global struggle between Islam and the West. For some members of the diaspora who felt alienated or discriminated against in their host countries, ISIS offered a radical but clear identity and a sense of belonging.

Political and social marginalization also played a significant role in diaspora's support for ISIS. In many Western countries, Muslim communities face discrimination, Islamophobia and social exclusion. These experiences of marginalization and the perception of Western governments oppressing or attacking Muslim countries can make some members of the diaspora receptive to ISIS's radical ideology.

ISIS cleverly exploited these feelings of marginalization by presenting itself as the defender of Muslims worldwide and calling on its followers to join the "holy war." The social isolation and lack of prospects experienced by many young Muslims in the diaspora became fertile ground for radicalization and support for extremist movements.

Emotional and family ties also played a role in diaspora's support for ISIS. Some members of the diaspora supported ISIS because they had relatives or friends who had joined the organization. In other cases, support has been provided under social pressure within the community or because of threats against family members in their home countries.

In some cases, families in the diaspora felt a moral obligation to support their relatives who were in ISIS areas, especially when they were in trouble or in need of support. These complex family ties often made it difficult for those affected to evade support, even if they were not personally convinced of ISIS's ideology.

The support of IS by members of the diaspora has had a significant impact on the affected communities, especially in Western countries. One of the most serious consequences was the increased stigma and discrimination to which Muslim communities were exposed. The association of Islam with terrorism, which was further reinforced by the actions of ISIS, led to a rise in Islamophobia and anti-Muslim rhetoric.

This stigma has had a negative impact on the lives of Muslims in the diaspora, including difficulties in finding work, social isolation, and a rise in hate crimes. Islamophobic crimes in Germany increased by 140% from 2022 to 2023. In addition, media reports about the involvement of diaspora members in ISIS contributed to mistrust of Muslim communities, which further hampered integration and community life.

The support of IS by diaspora members has led to a tightening of security laws and the surveillance of Muslim communities in many countries. Governments around the world introduced stricter measures to prevent ISIS recruitment and funding. This included monitoring mosques, charities and social networks, as well as imposing penalties on those suspected of supporting ISIS.

However, these security measures also led to tensions within Muslim communities and to the perception that they were being treated unfairly or placed under general suspicion. The resulting surveillance and controls often contributed to increasing feelings of marginalization, which in turn could encourage further radicalization.

In the long term, the support of IS by parts of the diaspora communities has led to a deep division within these communities. Many Muslims in the diaspora were forced to clearly distance themselves from the extremist elements, often leading to internal conflicts and tensions. At the same time, the relationship between the diaspora communities and the host countries has been permanently affected by the mistrust and security measures.

The need to promote dialogue and understanding within diaspora communities, as well as between these communities and the majority society, has been made even more urgent by these developments. A key challenge remains to find ways to prevent radicalisation while promoting integration and coexistence.

The diaspora's role in supporting the Islamic State was complex and multi-layered. Although only a small minority of the Muslim diaspora has actively contributed to supporting ISIS, their actions have had far-reaching consequences for the affected communities and their relations with host countries. Support came in various forms, including financial support, recruitment, propaganda, and ideological support, and was based on a mix of ideological beliefs, political and social marginalization, and emotional and family ties.

The impact of this support has been profound, both for the diaspora communities themselves and for their relationship with host countries. The challenges posed by these developments require continuous engagement with the root causes of radicalisation, the promotion of positive dialogue and the support of integration measures that are tailored to the specific needs and realities of the Muslim diaspora. Only through such a comprehensive and differentiated approach can it be possible to overcome divisions and strengthen resilience to extremist ideologies.

CHILD SOLDIERS AND IS: THE "CALF GENERATION"

The practice of using child soldiers in armed conflicts is a despicable phenomenon that has been observed throughout history in various regions of the world. The Islamic State (IS) was no exception. A particularly alarming development was the systematic recruitment and indoctrination of children, whom IS referred to as the "generation of calves". This practice served not only to strengthen his military ranks, but also to ensure ideological continuity.

The term "generation of calves" (Arabic: "Ashbal al-Khilafa", literally "the lion cubs of the caliphate") underlines ISIS's claim to raise a new generation that is socialized in its extremist ideology from birth. The "calves" were to become the fighters of tomorrow, educated to defend the caliphate and spread its values. The term also suggests the innocence and malleability of the children, who grew up from the beginning in an environment marked by violence, religious extremism and totalitarian control. The aim of this practice was to create a generation of children who knew no alternative reality and who were willing to fight and die for the ideals of ISIS.

ISIS took a multi-faceted approach to recruiting and indoctrinating children. Children were recruited both in the areas controlled by IS and from abroad. There were various mechanisms by which children got into the ranks of IS.

Recruitment in ISIS-controlled areas: In the regions it controls, especially Syria and Iraq, IS forced children and young people to join its ranks. Recruitment was often done by force, either directly through kidnappings or by putting pressure on the families. In many cases, it was orphans or children whose parents were killed or imprisoned who were particularly vulnerable to recruitment.

Indoctrination in schools and training camps: ISIS operated a network of schools and training camps in the areas under its control, where the children underwent intensive ideological training. The curriculum in these schools focused on the teachings of extremist Salafism, the legitimization of violence, and the glorification of martyrdom. In the training camps, the children received military training that included the use of weapons, hand-to-hand combat and the execution of suicide bombings. They were trained as full-fledged fighters, regardless of their age or emotional maturity.

Parenting by family members: In many cases, the children's parents or relatives played a key role in their radicalization. Families who had joined IS actively brought their children into the group's structures. These children grew up in an environment where the ideology of ISIS was taken for granted and absolute. Parents who entered the service of ISIS often saw the education of their children as a religious duty, which consisted of raising them as loyal followers of the caliphate.

IS brutally used children in military operations. This practice not only violated international human rights standards, but also had a profound impact on the children concerned.

Child soldiers in combat: Children were used as frontline combatants, often in particularly dangerous missions. They served as snipers, guards, and participants in attacks. Because they were easier to manipulate and less afraid of death, they were often sent into particularly risky situations.

Suicide bombings: The systematic training of children to become suicide bombers was particularly shocking. IS portrayed these children as "martyrs" who fought for Islam and the caliphate through their deaths. Children were sent to densely populated areas in cars or with explosive belts to blow themselves up and others. This practice was a particularly cynical expression of ISIS's willingness to sacrifice even the youngest for its goals.

Forced recruitment of minors for logistics and support: In addition to their role as fighters, children were also used for logistical tasks. They acted as couriers, spies and were trained in the production of explosives. In addition, they were often used as "human shields" to protect ISIS fighters and strategic positions.

The recruitment and use of children as soldiers and fighters had profound psychological and social consequences. Children who served in the ranks of ISIS were subjected to extreme physical and psychological stress. This led to severe trauma that shaped the entire rest of these children's lives.

Psychological trauma: Children who were deployed as soldiers often suffered from post-traumatic stress disorder (PTSD), depression, anxiety and other mental disorders. The constant contact with violence, the loss of family members and participation in killings left deep psychological wounds. These children often had difficulty returning to a normal life after the end of their time with IS and suffered from persistent mental health problems.

Alienation and social isolation: Children who grew up in the ranks of ISIS often had little contact with the outside world and grew up in an environment strongly influenced by ISIS's extremist teachings. In many cases, these children were isolated from society and had difficulty finding their place in society after the end of ISIS. Many of them were stigmatized and rejected in the communities to which they returned.

Childhood loss and education: Children recruited by ISIS often lost any opportunity for a normal childhood. They were kept out of school and instead received an "education" aimed solely at turning them into fighters. This loss of education and social experience made it difficult for them to lead a normal life and integrate into society after the end of their time with IS.

The international community has largely condemned ISIS's use of child soldiers and has sought to take measures to combat this phenomenon. The United Nations (UN) and various non-governmental organizations have launched programs to reintegrate child soldiers to provide them with psychological support and education.

Rehabilitation and reintegration: The reintegration of former child soldiers into society is an enormous challenge. Psychological care, schooling and social support are crucial to help these children process the traumatic experiences and lead a normal life. However, the return of child soldiers to their countries of origin, especially in Europe and North Africa, is often difficult because they are seen not only as victims but also as potential perpetrators.

Legal and political problems: Many countries are faced with the question of how to deal with returning child soldiers, especially those who have been involved in violent acts. The question of criminal responsibility poses a significant dilemma, as many of these children acted under duress or in a state of ideological blindness. International human rights organizations urge that these children be viewed primarily as victims and that measures be taken for reintegration and re-habilitation.

Preventive measures: Preventing the recruitment of child soldiers remains a key challenge. There is an urgent need for comprehensive measures that include not only military but also social, economic and political approaches. This includes tackling poverty, creating educational opportunities and promoting social inclusion to combat the environment that leads to the radicalisation of children.

WOMEN IN THE ISLAMIC STATE: ROLE, IDEOLOGY AND RECRUITMENT

However, a lesser noticed but extremely important dimension of his organization was the role of women. Women played a complex and often contradictory role within ISIS, which was determined both ideologically and practically by the jihadist interpretation of Islam. While they were to remain largely invisible to the public, their recruitment, indoctrination and active participation in the structures of the caliphate was a central part of ISIS's strategy.

ISIS's ideology regarding women was based on an extremist, Salafist interpretation of Islam, which was based on an ultra-conservative interpretation of Sharia. In this understanding, women were seen as subordinate members of society, whose main tasks were to perform domestic duties, give birth to children, and support their male relatives in jihad. This patriarchal idea of gender roles was central to the maintenance of social order within the caliphate.

Women were assigned a dual role: on the one hand, they were seen as "protectors" of jihadist ideology, whose job was to educate and indoctrinate the next generation of fighters. On the other hand, they were also victims of systematic oppression and control, especially in the form of strict dress codes, movement restrictions and forced marriages.

IS propagated an image of women that was strongly based on the role of wife and mother. Women were to play a central role in the continuation of the caliphate by giving birth to and raising children, especially sons. These children should be shaped from birth in the spirit of the ideology of IS to secure the next generation of fighters. "Holy Motherhood" was strongly idealized in the propaganda of IS. Women fulfilling their roles as mothers and wives were seen as crucial to the long-term success of the caliphate.

Within this patriarchal structure, the role of women was also portrayed as a form of ideological warfare: while men fought on the front line, women were supposed to stabilize the caliphate from within. The birth and upbringing of many children was considered a religious and political duty. Women who accepted and fulfilled this role were portrayed as morally superior, while women who resisted this order or questioned the traditional role were considered apostate or un-Islamic.

Although the role of women was primarily limited to the domestic sphere, in some cases they were also used in military and administrative functions. Particularly noteworthy was the creation of the so-called "Al-Khansaa Brigade", all-female religious police. This brigade was responsible for monitoring and enforcing the strict dress codes and codes of conduct imposed by ISIS on women. Women from this brigade patrolled the streets of ISIS-controlled areas and made sure that other women followed Islamic norms as interpreted by ISIS.

The existence of the Al-Khansaa Brigade makes it clear that women in ISIS were not only passive victims but were also actively involved in maintaining the order of the caliphate. The members of this brigade had considerable power over other women and were responsible for punishments for violations of the strict rules of conduct. These positions of power offered some women the opportunity to rise within the jihadist hierarchy, even if they remained subject to ideological subordination to men.

The recruitment of women has been a central part of ISIS's global strategy. Western women and women from Muslim countries were targeted by propaganda that painted an idealized picture of life in the caliphate. ISIS portrayed life in the caliphate as spiritually fulfilling and a way to live Islam in its "purest" form without being influenced by Western or secular values.

Propaganda and social media: ISIS used social media and online platforms extensively to recruit women worldwide. Professionally produced videos, blogs and magazines such as "Dabiq" and "Rumiyah" aimed to portray life in the caliphate as utopian and morally superior. Women were encouraged by emotional and religious appeals to follow the call of the caliphate and settle in Syria or Iraq. They should see themselves as wives of fighters, mothers and educators of the next generation of jihadists.

Roles in the diaspora: Women in the Muslim diaspora in Europe and North America were also specifically addressed. Many women who grew up in these countries suffered from identity crises, discrimination and the feeling of alienation from their surroundings. IS offered them a supposedly clear and morally superior identity and promised a community in which they could live their religious convictions freely. The propaganda highlighted the role of women as part of a global struggle that was waged not only on the battlefield, but also in homes and families.

Coercion and manipulation: In addition to voluntary recruitment, IS also relied on coercion and manipulation. Women living in the areas controlled by IS often had no choice but to adapt to jihadist structures. Many women were forced into marriage, often to foreign fighters who had come to the region to join ISIS. These women had little control over their lives and were victims of a system that reduced them to their role as wives and mothers.

A particularly dark chapter in the role of women in ISIS concerns the widespread sexual violence that has been systematically used against women. Non-Muslim women, such as Yazidi women, were considered "spoils of war" and enslaved in large numbers. This practice was firmly anchored in the jihadist ideology of ISIS, which religiously justified such forms of enslavement and rape. ISIS justified the enslavement of women as a revival of a practice that was supposedly allowed in the early days of Islam. Yazidi women were captured in large numbers, sold and abused as sex slaves.

Sexual violence was a systematic part of ISIS's warfare, serving both as a means of rewarding fighters and oppressing the non-Muslim population. Many women were forced to enter several marriages, whereby they were immediately assigned to another fighter after the death of their "husband". This practice left traumatized victims and led to international outrage.

It is important to emphasize that women in ISIS acted both as victims and perpetrators. Many women were drawn into or forced into the structures of IS and had little control over their own fate. Others, however, actively participated in the implementation of jihadist ideology. They helped monitor other women, were involved in recruitment, and supported the caliphate in a variety of ways.

This dual function as victims and perpetrators makes it difficult to assess the role of women in IS. Many of the women who lived in the areas controlled by ISIS were forced to adapt to the jihadist system to survive. Others, on the other hand, actively sought ways to gain power within this system and consciously contributed to the maintenance of the extremist order.

The question of the return of women who have joined ISIS is a significant challenge. Many of these women returned to their countries of origin after the fall of the caliphate, especially to Europe, North Africa and Central Asia. The societies to which they returned were faced with the difficult task of deciding how to deal with these women.

The prosecution of women who joined ISIS varies from country to country. Some countries consider these women criminals and terrorists and prosecute them accordingly. Other countries see them more as victims, especially if they have entered the structures of IS under duress or deception.

THE FINANCING OF TERROR: ECONOMIC FOUNDATIONS OF THE ISLAMIC STATE

In recent years, the Islamic State has been one of the most dangerous terrorist organizations, whose financial infrastructure has allowed it to plan and conduct large-scale operations and control areas. ISIS's ability to finance itself has been a key to its power and influence. Unlike many other terrorist organizations, which rely heavily on external donations, ISIS developed a diversified and self-sufficient financing model that relied on controlling territory, exploiting resources, and extorting local populations.

The roots of ISIS's financing model can be traced back to the time of Al-Qaeda in Iraq (AQI), ISIS's predecessor organization. AQI, under the leadership of Abu Musab al-Zarqawi, was financed mainly by donations from supporters abroad, especially from the Gulf States. However, this dependence on external donors also brought vulnerabilities, as financing was highly dependent on political support and economic conditions in donor countries.

With the creation of ISIS, and especially after the conquest of large areas in Iraq and Syria, the group developed a complex financing model that enabled it to operate largely independently of external donations. By controlling areas with significant economic resources, ISIS has been able to create a wide range of revenue streams.

A central element of ISIS's financing model was territorial control. By conquering and administering territories in Iraq and Syria, IS was able to access the economic resources available there and establish a kind of "shadow governorate". This control allowed ISIS to levy taxes and levies, regulate trade, and use local industries to generate revenue.

The administration of these territories was carried out according to a strict bureaucratic model aimed at maximizing revenues. ISIS established a comprehensive tax and contribution system that covered all aspects of economic life in the occupied territories. At the same time, the organization-controlled access to basic services such as water, electricity, and security, which allowed it to effectively blackmail the local population.

One of the most important sources of income for IS was the illegal trade in oil. After the conquest of oil fields in Iraq and Syria, ISIS began to systematically exploit these resources. The group operated several oil fields, refineries and transport routes that allowed it to sell crude oil both locally and internationally.

The oil was often sold at a greatly reduced price on the black market, making ISIS a major player in the illicit oil market. Buyers were both local smugglers and international buyers, including some who concealed the origin of the oil to circumvent sanctions. Revenues from the oil trade were estimated to be several million dollars per day at peak times, forming the backbone of ISIS financing.

Another significant element of ISIS funding was the sophisticated system of taxes and duties that the organization implemented in the areas under its control. ISIS levied taxes on almost all economic activities, including trade, agriculture and services. In addition, special "protection money" was demanded from minorities and wealthy individuals who did not follow the group's jihadist ideologies.

The "jizya", a historic poll tax for non-Muslim residents, was also reintroduced in the areas controlled by ISIS, forcing religious minorities to pay significant sums to continue living in their homes. These measures led to considerable financial exploitation of the local population and contributed significantly to the economic stability of IS.

Extortion was another essential means of financing ISIS. The group took advantage of the insecurity and chaos in the areas under its control to systematically collect extortion money from companies, wealthy individuals and even aid organizations. Companies were forced to pay "protection money" to continue operating, while individuals were often threatened with violence or kidnapping to force payments.

Kidnappings also played an important role in financing ISIS. Both foreigners and locals have been kidnapped to extort ransom. These kidnappings were often directed against journalists, aid workers and members of religious minorities. In some cases, ISIS demanded millions in ransom, with failure to pay often resulting in public executions, which in turn were used as propaganda.

Looting and raids were other significant sources of income for ISIS, especially in the early stages of its expansion. After conquering territory, ISIS systematically looted state and private institutions, including banks, administrative buildings and military camps. The most spectacular of these raids was the capture of the Iraqi city of Mosul, in which IS is estimated to have stolen up to 500 million US dollars from the banks there.

These funds were immediately invested in warfare and in the administration of the conquered territories, which allowed ISIS to consolidate and further expand its power. Art treasures and antiques that were stolen in the conquered territories were also sold on the black market and contributed to financing.

Although IS primarily relied on internal sources of income, the group also benefited indirectly from international humanitarian aid. In the conflict-affected areas, especially in Syria, IS managed to intercept parts of the aid deliveries or control their distribution. By controlling these resources, ISIS was not only able to influence the local population, but also to sell humanitarian goods on the black market.

In addition, there are indications that ISIS has also used international remittances to obtain funds from supporters abroad. These funds often flowed through opaque channels that were difficult to trace, such as informal remittance systems ("hawala") or through legal banking systems used by front organizations.

ISIS's extensive financial resources have been used mainly to finance its military apparatus. ISIS had a well-equipped army armed with both light and heavy weapons, including captured modern equipment. The group used its financial resources to purchase weapons, ammunition and military equipment, and operated extensive logistics to supply its troops in the occupied territories. In addition, a significant part of the financial

IS 2015 revenue Figures in millions of USD

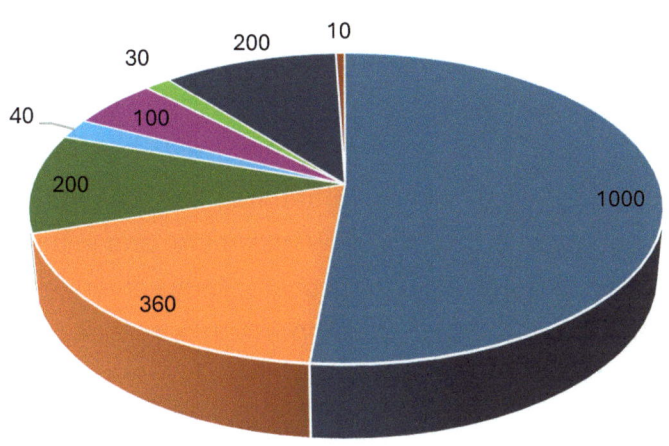

- Oil sales
- Looting and robbery
- Antiquity and cultural assets
- Agriculture and trade
- Blackmail and protection money
- Human trafficking
- Donations from abroad
- Digital crime

resources were used to recruit and pay fighters. ISIS offered its fighters comparatively high salaries, which helped to create a loyal and motivated force. In addition, incentives such as loot and the prospect of power and influence in the occupied territories were offered.

THE IMPORTANCE OF SYMBOLS AND RITUALS IN THE ISLAMIC STATE

The Islamic State has distinguished itself not only for its brutal military tactics and strict ideology, but also for its deliberate use of symbols and rituals that are deeply embedded in its identity and strategy. These symbols and rituals played a central role in the self-definition of IS and its followers, in the recruitment and radicalization of new members, and in the mobilization of supporters on a global scale. They served not only to strengthen the community of supporters, but also to unsettle and intimidate the enemies of IS.

IS leaned heavily on religious and historical symbols and rituals to present itself as the legitimate successor of early Islam and the restorer of a "pure" caliphate. The return to the beginnings of Islam and the link to prophetic traditions served to legitimize the ideology of IS and to emphasize the continuity between the beginnings of Islam and its own movement.

A central aspect of ISIS's ideological foundation was the idea of jihad as a holy war, supported and consecrated by religious symbols and rituals. The use of symbols such as the black flag of ISIS, which is traced back to the flag of the Prophet Mohammed, or the practice of public executions as ritual purification, underline the group's claim to act in accordance with the divine order.

The caliphate is a central symbol in ISIS's ideology and represents the unity and leadership of the Muslim ummah (community). IS claimed to restore the caliphate, which was founded after the death of the Prophet Muhammad. By proclaiming the caliphate in 2014 and symbolically appointing Abu Bakr al-Baghdadi as caliph, ISIS sought to establish its religious and political authority over all Muslims worldwide.

The caliphate was not only a political construct, but also a powerful symbol of the restoration of a "just" Islamic order, which in the eyes of ISIS had been lost in the modern age. It served as a unified symbol for recruiting followers who felt alienated from the existing political systems and were looking for a radical alternative.

One of the most recognizable symbols of ISIS is the black flag, widely known as the "Banner of the Caliphate" or the "Banner of Jihad." The flag shows the Islamic creed ("Shahada") in white lettering on a black background and a round seal symbolizing the Prophet Mohammed. This symbol is deliberately used to make the connection to early Islam and the original jihadist movement.

The black flag serves both as an identity marker for IS and as a demonstration of power. It can be seen on numerous propaganda videos, official announcements and at public appearances by IS fighters. The spread of  the flag, especially in areas conquered by ISIS, symbolized the group's rule and was intended to remind the population that ISIS represents the true caliphate.

Another central symbol of IS is the "Shahada" finger-pointing, in which a follower raises his index finger to testify to the unity of God and the Islamic creed. This symbol was widely used in ISIS propaganda and served as a visual sign of loyalty to  ISIS's ideology and its vision of a theocratic state.

The "Shahada" finger pointing is often shown in propaganda images and videos to underline the unity and zeal of the fighters. This symbol became a distinguishing feature for ISIS supporters and helped create a visual identity that connected followers worldwide and reinforced the sense of belonging and shared mission.

The public executions that IS recorded on video and distributed worldwide represent a particularly gruesome form of symbolism. These videos were not only acts of extreme violence, but also deeply ritualized and symbolically charged acts that were placed in the context of the "holy war".

Executions, especially by beheading, were presented as ritual acts supposedly justified by religious texts. These acts served as a show of force and intimidation tactics and were aimed at spreading fear among ISIS's enemies, while at the same time showcasing the group's power and determination. The victims were often referred to as "infidels" or "traitors," which made ISIS portray its acts of violence as divinely justified.

Rituals played an important role in the recruitment and indoctrination of new members of ISIS. The handing over of the black flag, taking an oath of allegiance (Bay'ah) to the Caliph and participating in religious ceremonies glorifying martyrdom were central elements that strengthened the identity and cohesion of the group.

The oath of allegiance was a particularly significant ritual that symbolically marked the transition of a recruit from an ordinary Muslim to a "true believer" and fighter of the caliphate. This oath was not only an act of loyalty, but also an act of self-commitment to a life in the service of the caliphate and, if necessary, to death in battle.

The concept of martyrdom (shahada) played a central role in ISIS's ideology and was supported by specific rituals.

Potential martyrs were often honored in ritual ceremonies where their upcoming mission was presented as a sacred act. These rituals included prayers, the reading of religious texts, and symbolic acts that emphasized the act of sacrifice as an act pleasing to God.

Martyrs were hailed as heroes in ISIS propaganda after their deaths, which glorified their actions and encouraged others to emulate them. ISIS used these rituals to create a culture of martyrdom that was deeply embedded in the organization's ideology and fostered a constant readiness for sacrifice and jihad.

ISIS also carried out a series of public punishment rituals that were highly ritualistic and symbolically charged. These punishments, which often included corporal punishment such as flogging, amputation, or stoning, were presented as "divine justice" and were intended to enforce Sharia law.

The public nature of these punishments served to demonstrate the power of ISIS and to discipline the population. They were designed to create fear and obedience, reinforcing the message that ISIS was the absolute authority in the areas it controlled. Such rituals were not only acts of punishment, but also of control and intimidation.

ISIS symbols and rituals played a crucial role in mobilizing and radicalizing supporters worldwide. The clear and recognizable symbols, such as the black flag or the shahada finger point, allowed followers to identify with the movement, regardless of where they were. These symbols served as visual bridges that conveyed the sense of a global community connected by jihad.

The ritualization of violence and martyrdom motivated individuals to join ISIS by providing religious and moral justification for their actions. Propaganda videos showing these rituals acted as powerful tools of indoctrination, encouraging potential recruits to follow the "sacred" path of jihad.

ISIS symbols and rituals also had a strong effect on psychological warfare. The deliberate use of violence enshrined in rituals and the dissemination of these acts through propaganda channels were intended to intimidate both opponents and the international community. The symbolic power of these actions lay in their ability to generate fear and resignation, underscoring ISIS's resilience and willingness to take extreme measures.

This psychological warfare was designed to demoralize the enemy and break the support of the population in the affected areas. By using rituals and symbols as tools of fear and submission, IS was able to effectively enforce and consolidate its rule.

The importance of symbols and rituals in the Islamic State cannot be underestimated. They played a central role in the creation and maintenance of the ideological, social and military structure of the group. Through the deliberate and strategic use of religious and historical symbols, as well as through the ritualization of violence and loyalty, IS was able to build a strong identity that tied followers to itself and intimidated opponents.

These symbols and rituals allowed ISIS to create a coherent and assertive movement, capable of mobilizing a global base of supporters and weakening its enemies through psychological means. Although IS is largely defeated militarily today, its symbols and rituals remain anchored in the minds of many people and continue to act as a reminder of the power that the Islamic State once had.

IS AND THE DESTRUCTION OF CULTURAL HERITAGE: AN IDEOLOGICAL STRATEGY?

The destruction of cultural heritage by the Islamic State (IS) is one of the most devastating aspects of the jihadist campaign in the Middle East. Historical sites, archaeological finds and religious monuments that had survived for thousands of years were systematically destroyed by IS. The destruction in cities such as Palmyra, Nimrud and Mosul shocked the world and led to international outrage. However, this destruction is not only an expression of vandalism, but part of an ideological strategy that is deeply rooted in the jihadist worldview of ISIS

In the context of Salafist ideology, the destruction of cultural assets by IS can be understood as a radical rejection of history that is not in harmony with Islam. ISIS propagated the idea that all forms of worship or respect for cultural and religious symbols outside Islam are to be regarded as shirk (polytheism). For ISIS, the destruction of historical sites, especially those associated with pre-Islamic civilizations or "wrong" religious practices, was a means of erasing these cultural traces.

ISIS particularly targeted places that symbolized the region's cultural and religious diversity, such as the ruins of Palmyra in Syria, which were known for their Roman and Hellenistic influences. These places posed a challenge for ISIS, as they were seen as symbols of a non-Islamic past that were to be erased from the collective memory by the creation of the "caliphate".

Palmyra: The ancient oasis city of Palmyra, known for its Roman temples, columns, and theaters, was captured by ISIS fighters in 2015. The city was not only an important cultural heritage of Syria, but also a UNESCO World Heritage Site. ISIS destroyed numerous monuments, including the Temple of Baal and the Temple of Bel, which were considered symbols of pagan idolatry. The media-effective blowing up of these monuments served not only the religious "cleansing", but also the global staging of the power of IS.

Nimrud and Nineveh: In Iraq, ISIS also destroyed important archaeological sites from the time of the Assyrian Empire, including Nimrud and Nineveh, which are among the oldest civilizational centers of humanity. The destruction of statues, reliefs and architectural monuments in these sites was carried out partly by targeted blasting and partly using heavy machinery. These actions were also ideologically justified and were intended to erase the traces of the pre-Islamic civilizations of the Middle East.

Al-Nuri Mosque in Mosul: Although the destruction of pre-Islamic sites was in the foreground, IS also attacked religious sites that can be attributed to Islam itself if they did not correspond to the jihadist ideas of IS. An emblematic example is the destruction of the Al-Nuri Mosque in Mosul, which dates to the 12th century and was known for its leaning minaret. IS blew up the mosque in 2017, shortly before Iraqi forces recaptured Mosul. This destruction symbolized ISIS's refusal to accept religious institutions that did not conform to its own version of Islam.

The destruction of cultural heritage by IS was not only an expression of vandalism or religious fanaticism, but also a deliberate ideological strategy. This strategy had several objectives:

Religious purity: The destruction of cultural assets served IS to create a symbolic separation between the past and the "pure" Islamic future it propagated. By destroying religious and cultural sites associated with pre-Islamic or "deviant" Islamic traditions, ISIS presented itself as the preserver of an "authentic" Islam. This idea of religious purity was central to the legitimation of the "caliphate" and was intended to demonstrate the religious and moral superiority of IS over its enemies.

Propaganda and intimidation: The destruction of cultural heritage also had a propaganda purpose. The media dissemination of images and videos of the destruction was an instrument of intimidation and the spread of fear. IS used the destruction to demonstrate its power and determination and to provoke the Western world and the international community. The destruction of sites that were considered the cultural heritage of humanity symbolized the rejection of the global order and the values associated with that order.

Economic motives: In addition to ideological and propaganda motives, IS also pursued economic goals. While IS publicly destroyed certain cultural assets, it looted other objects and sold them on the black market. The proceeds from the illegal trade in antiquities were used to finance the terrorist organization. This contradiction – the simultaneous destruction and trade in cultural property – makes it clear that ISIS's actions were not only ideologically but also pragmatically motivated.

ISIS's destruction of cultural heritage is part of a broader pattern that can also be observed in other extremist movements. Attacking cultural and religious sites is a strategy that aims to undermine identities and destroy the social coherence of communities. By attacking cultural assets, extremist groups attack the symbols and memories that are central to the cultural self-image of societies.

In the case of ISIS, the destruction served not only to carry out a religious "cleansing", but also to propagate the idea of a global Islamic community that has freed itself from any pre-Islamic and "un-Islamic" influences. This idea of a "pure" Islam, asserting itself against the influence of history and Western modernity, is at the heart of the ideology of ISIS and similar extremist movements.

DEVELOPMENT OF THE WEAPONS USED BY IS IN EUROPE

The terrorist attacks in Europe, which have been carried out in the name of the Islamic State since 2014, have had a major impact on the security situation on the continent. An important component of these attacks is the choice of the weapons used by terrorists.

In the period from 2014 to 2023, a clear development in the type of weapons used can be observed, ranging from firearms and explosives to less conventional means such as knives and vehicles. This analysis sheds light on the different types of weapons used in terrorist attacks by IS supporters or sympathizers in Europe and examines the background to the change in the choice of weapons in crime.

Since ISIS's self-proclamation of the caliphate in 2014, several attacks have been carried out in Europe in the name of the terrorist organization. The earliest attacks were mainly carried out by returnees from combat zones in Syria and Iraq who were trained in the use of firearms and explosives. Later, however, more and more lone perpetrators were radicalized who operated without a direct connection to the organization, which also had an impact on the choice of murder weapons.

Between 2014 and 2017, firearms and explosives dominated as weapons of crime in the largest and most devastating attacks. The perpetrators were often well-trained and had connections to networks in the combat zones of the Middle East.

The attacks in Paris in November 2015, in which 130 people died, were carried out with Kalashnikov assault rifles and explosive vests. These weapons showed the ability of terrorists to obtain weapons of war and use them in urban areas.

Like the Paris attacks, firearms and explosives were also used in Brussels. The terrorists used homemade explosive devices and attacked the airport and a subway station.
The use of such weapons illustrates the ability of IS in this phase to plan complex, coordinated attacks with high logistical effort.

The availability of weapons of war, especially assault rifles, and access to explosive chemicals posed major challenges for security agencies in Europe. It was found that criminal networks often acted as intermediaries for weapons and explosives, which facilitated procurement.

After 2017, the pattern of the murder weapons used changed significantly. The increasing defeat of IS in Syria and Iraq as well as the increased monitoring and disruption of terrorist networks in Europe are making access to heavy weapons and explosives more difficult. This led to an increased use of lighter, improvised weapons that were easier to obtain and more discreet to use.

Knives have increasingly become the weapon of choice for IS sympathizers in Europe because they are readily available, inconspicuous and easy to handle. Many of the attackers were lone perpetrators who were radicalized by online propaganda.

A well-known example is the attack on Westminster Bridge, in which a lone perpetrator ran over people with a vehicle and then injured several people with a knife.

In this attack, the perpetrator first ran over people with a truck before attacking other people with a knife. This attack shows the increasing use of everyday objects such as vehicles in conjunction with knives.

From 2016 onwards, there were several attacks in which vehicles were used as the main weapon. This method is particularly devastating because it is difficult to predict and can be carried out with little effort. Access to vehicles is almost unhindered in Europe, which made this weapon particularly attractive to terrorists.

A van was driven into a crowd of people on Barcelona's famous Ramblas, resulting in numerous deaths and injuries. Such attacks illustrate the ease with which terrorists can turn inconspicuous vehicles into deadly weapons.

Although there have been no major successful attacks with chemical or biological weapons in Europe, there was an incident in Cologne in 2018 in which a radicalized IS sympathizer tried to prepare an attack using ricin, a potent poison. This incident shows that despite the difficulty of obtaining and producing such weapons, ISIS sympathizers have tried to use chemical and biological means for terrorist purposes.

After the major attacks in 2015 and 2016, the European security authorities tightened their measures to prevent terrorist attacks. Border controls, surveillance of returnees from combat zones and stricter gun laws made heavier weapons such as assault rifles and explosives more difficult to obtain.

IS propaganda on social media played an important role in the radicalization of lone perpetrators. The group called on sympathizers to carry out attacks with simple means, such as knives or vehicles, if they did not have access to more complex weapons.

While in the early phases many attackers had direct connections to IS, this increasingly changed after 2017. Lone perpetrators who lived in Europe and became radicalized via the Internet increased. These individuals rarely had access to the same resources as the earlier returnees from the war zones, which encouraged the use of simple weapons.

The development of the weapons used from 2014 to 2023 reflects the changing dynamics of international terrorism. While the early attacks relied on heavy weapons and complex networks, improvised weapons such as knives and vehicles have been preferred over the years. This shift is the result of increased security measures, the dismantling of IS networks in the Middle East and the radicalization of lone perpetrators in Europe. The choice of weapons during this period also illustrates the flexibility and adaptability of IS and its supporters. It remains a challenge for European security agencies to identify and prevent new threats, especially at a time when terrorists are increasingly resorting to simple but equally lethal means.

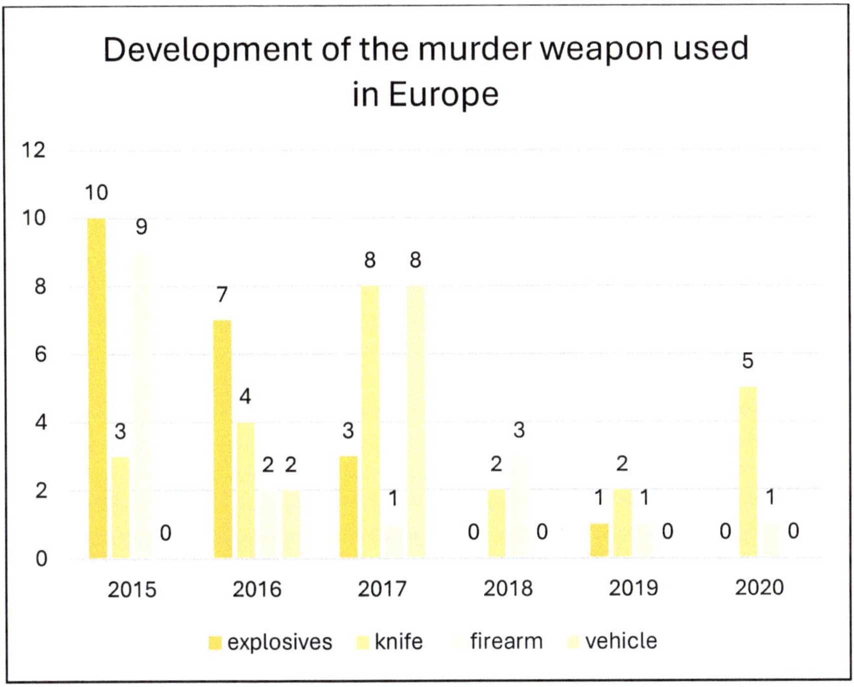

Development of the murder weapon used in Europe
12
10
8
6
4
2
0
10
9
3
0
7
4
2 2
3
8 8
1
0
2
3
0
1
2
1
0
0
5
1
0
2015
2016
2017
2018
2019
2020
explosives
knife
firearm
vehicle

Frequency of murder weapons used in IS attacks in Europe 2015-2020
30
25
20
15
10
5
0
15
24
19
11
Firearms
Knife
Explosive
Vehicle
frequency of murder weapons used in Europe

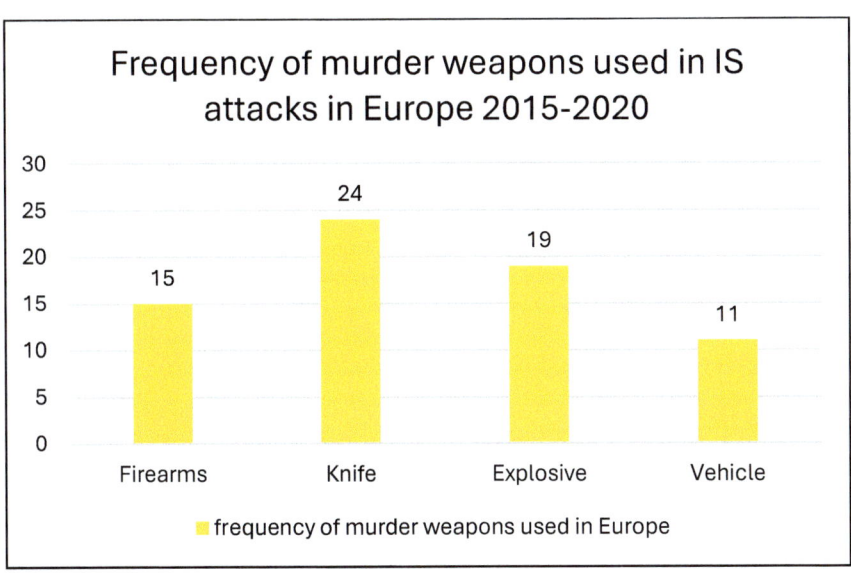

ISLAMIC STATE ATTACKS WORLDWIDE

Middle East, Iraq and Syria:
Iraq and Syria were the main areas of operation of IS. During its territorial peak (2014-2017), the group regularly carried out attacks to attack both military and civilian targets.

Baghdad, Iraq (2016): One of the most serious attacks by ISIS outside of Europe occurred on July 3, 2016, when a car bomb exploded in a busy shopping district in the Karrada district. More than 300 people were killed. The attack was aimed at stoking sectarian tensions between Sunnis and Shiites.

Homs and Damascus, Syria (2017): On February 25, 2017, ISIS carried out a double suicide bombing in Homs, killing 42 people, including high-ranking security officials. On October 11, 2017, ISIS attacked a police headquarters in Damascus to destabilize the government and spread fear among the residents of the capital.

Yemen: In Yemen, ISIS was particularly active in the cities of Aden and Sanaa, where it became embroiled in a bloody conflict with al-Qaeda in the Arabian Peninsula (AQAP).
Aden (2015): On 6 October 2015, ISIS carried out four suicide bombings in Aden, targeting security forces and a hotel where government officials were staying, killing 15 people.

Nigeria: ISIS has wreaked havoc in the region through the Islamic State in West Africa (ISWAP) group, a breakaway from Boko Haram.

Maiduguri (2016): On March 16, 2016, suicide bombers attacked a mosque in Maiduguri, killing over 25 people. The aim was to exacerbate religious tensions and further destabilize the government.

Egypt: In Egypt, ISIS has carried out numerous attacks, particularly in the Sinai Peninsula, targeting security forces and the Coptic Christian minority.

Sinai (2017): The attack on the al-Rawda Mosque on November 24, 2017, in which over 300 people were killed, was the deadliest in Egypt's modern history. The attack was directed against a Sufi community that IS considered un-Islamic.

Libya: Libya, which plunged into chaos after the fall of Gaddafi, became another important operational space for ISIS.

Tripoli (2015): On January 27, 2015, ISIS fighters attacked the Corinthia Hotel in Tripoli, a popular destination for diplomats and businessmen. Nine people were killed, including five foreigners.

Afghanistan: The IS offshoot "Islamic State in Khorasan Province" (IS-K) carried out numerous bloody attacks in Afghanistan and Pakistan.

Kabul (2021): On August 26, 2021, IS-K carried out a suicide attack at Kabul airport during the evacuation after the Taliban takeover. 170 Afghans and 13 US soldiers were killed. The attack was aimed at creating chaos and hitting the international community.

Pakistan:

In Pakistan, IS has increasingly targeted religious minorities such as Shiites and Sufis in recent years.

Quetta (2019): On April 12, 2019, a bomb exploded in a busy market district of Quetta, inhabited mainly by the Shiite Hazara community. 20 people were killed. The aim was to ignite sectarian violence and further destabilize the government.

Bangladesh:

ISIS began to cooperate with the local group "Jamaat-ul-Mujahideen Bangladesh" (JMB) in Bangladesh.

Dhaka (2016): On July 1, 2016, five ISIS terrorists stormed the Holey Artisan Bakery Café in Dhaka, killing 22 people, including 17 foreigners. The attack was aimed at unsettling the international community and consolidating ISIS's influence in South Asia.

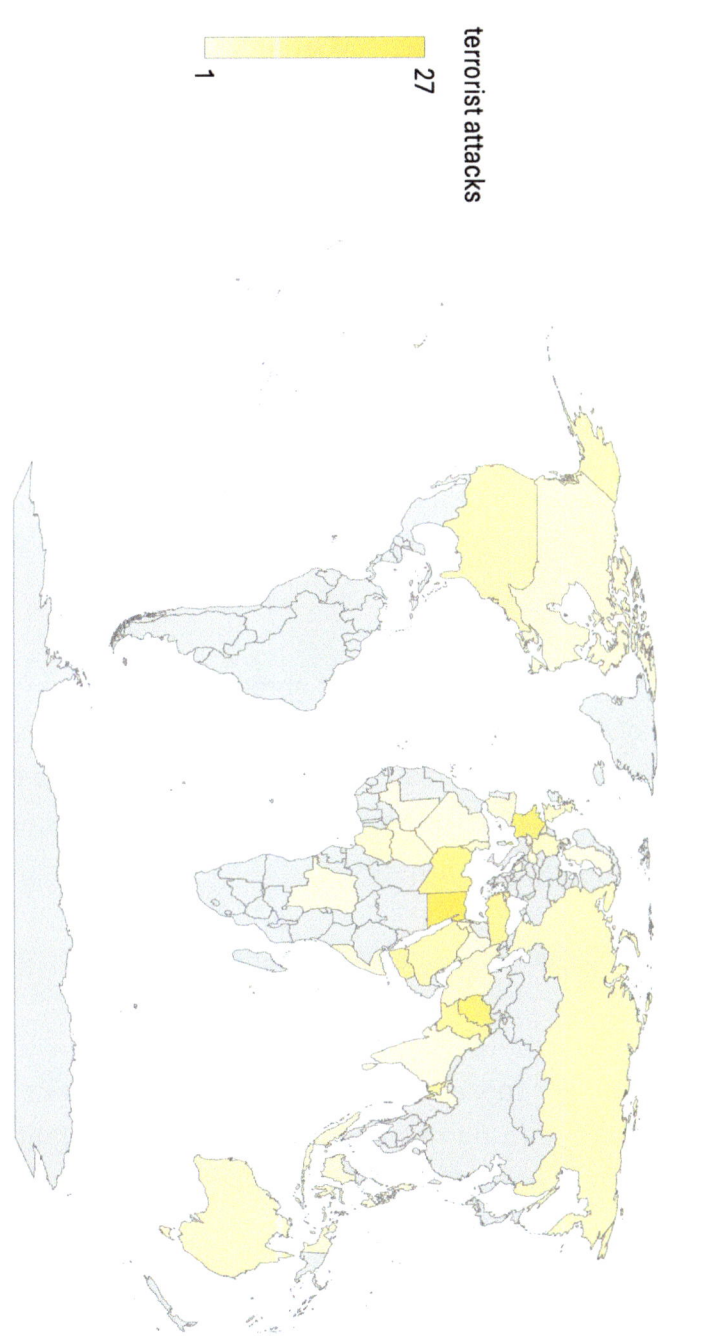

Map of IS attacks: Global distribution and frequency

terrorist attacks

1 — 27

Political and strategic goals

ISIS aims to foment political instability and undermine state structures to exploit the power vacuum and recruit new followers. In countries such as Iraq, Syria and Libya, ISIS took advantage of the weakness of governments and the chaotic situation to control territories and spread its ideology.

Religious and ideological goals

IS aims at religious cleansing and the creation of a homogeneous Islamist society. In countries such as Egypt and Afghanistan, religious minorities have been targeted to spread fear and exacerbate religious tensions.

Psychological warfare

Another aspect of the attacks is the spread of terror and fear among the civilian population. This is done through particularly brutal and public attacks, which serve to demoralize the population and reinforce the perception of the powerlessness of governments.

ISIS uses various tactics to spread maximum destruction and fear:

Suicide bombings: These are among the preferred tactics as they cause maximum damage and attract media attention. The attacks often target markets, mosques or military installations.

Booby Traps (IEDs): The use of improvised explosive devices, especially on roads and in urban areas, is a commonly used method of hitting security forces and civilians.

Hostage-taking and mass shootings: In countries such as Syria and Libya, numerous hostage-taking and mass executions have been carried out to terrorize the population and eliminate political opponents.

Coordinated attacks: ISIS often carries out coordinated attacks with several suicide bombers and gunmen to overwhelm the efficiency of the security forces and cause maximum damage.

Humanitarian impact

The IS attacks have led to massive humanitarian crises. Millions of people have been displaced, especially in Iraq and Syria, where the attacks often rendered entire villages and towns uninhabitable. The targeted attacks on religious minorities led to ethnic cleansing and genocide, as in the case of the Yazidis in Iraq.

Political and social impact

The attacks by IS have led to an aggravation of the security situation and a militarization of society in many countries. Governments responded with repressive measures, which often led to human rights violations. In countries such as Afghanistan and Libya, IS has increased political instability and significantly hampered the peace process.

The global attacks of the Islamic State have shown that the group poses a significant threat despite its territorial losses. Their ability to plan and carry out terrorist attacks is based on a well-connected structure and an ideology that extends far beyond the geographical borders of the Middle East. The long-term effects of these attacks are still being felt in many regions of the world and require continued vigilance and cooperation at the international level to sustainably weaken ISIS's influence and stabilize the affected communities.

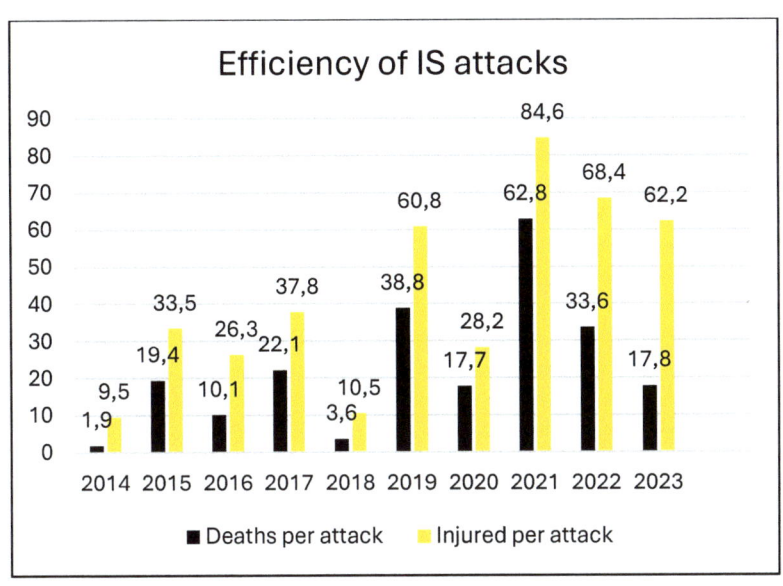

Efficiency of IS attacks

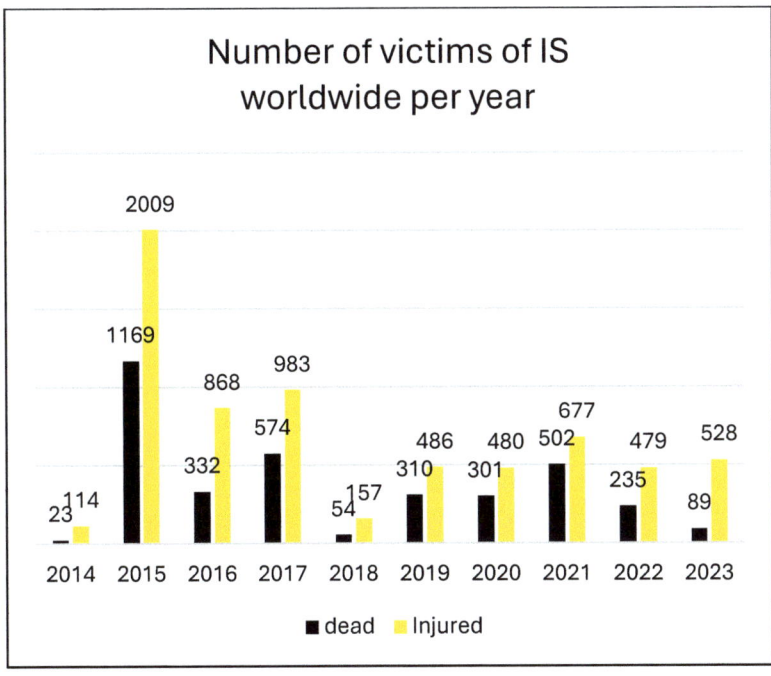

Number of victims of IS worldwide per year

ATTACKS BY THE ISLAMIC STATE IN EUROPE

Since its rise, the Islamic State (IS) has hit not only the Middle East but also Europe hard with a series of terrorist attacks. These attacks are aimed at spreading fear, destabilizing societies, and furthering the group's political and religious goals. ISIS's decision to target Europe is both strategic and ideologically motivated. For IS, Europe is symbolic of Western values that contradict its extremist interpretation of Islam. By attacking European cities, ISIS aims to:

Exert political pressure: European support for military interventions in the Middle East is to be undermined.
Spreading fear and insecurity: Terrorist attacks aim to shake the sense of security of the European population.
Promote propaganda: Successful attacks increase the group's attractiveness to potential recruits worldwide.

The attacks in Europe were often carried out by "lone wolves" or small cells that were either directly inspired by ISIS or supported by the organization. The attacks include a wide range of tactics, including gun attacks, explosive attacks, vehicular attacks, and knife attacks.

The following list offers examples of attacks by IS in Europe.

Brussels, Belgium (May 24, 2014) Attack on the Jewish Museum: A gunman opened fire at the Jewish Museum of Belgium in Brussels, killing four people. The perpetrator, Mehdi

Nemmouche, a French jihadist, had previously been in Syria and had ties to IS. This attack is considered one of the first in Europe to be carried out by a returnee from Syria. He highlighted the threat posed by "foreign fighters" who could carry out attacks in Europe.

Paris, France (7–9 January 2015) Charlie Hebdo and the supermarket attack: Two armed men broke into the office of the satirical magazine Charlie Hebdo and killed 12 people. Another attacker killed four people in a kosher supermarket on January 9. The attackers declared their loyalty to IS and Al-Qaeda. These attacks marked the beginning of a new wave of terrorist attacks in Europe. The attack on Charlie Hebdo was particularly symbolic, as it was staged in retaliation for the publication of caricatures of the Prophet Muhammad. He also showed how ideological motives led to the selection of targets.

Paris, France (November 13, 2015) Coordinated attacks in Paris: A series of bombings and shootings shook Paris. The attacks on the Stade de France, the Bataclan theatre and several cafés claimed 130 lives and injured over 350. The attackers were part of a well-organized cell that had ties to IS. This coordinated attack demonstrated ISIS's ability to conduct complex terrorist operations outside the Middle East. It was one of the deadliest attacks in the history of Europe and had far-reaching implications for European security policy.

Brussels, Belgium (22 March 2016) Attacks on the airport and metro: Two bomb explosions shook Brussels airport, and another bomb exploded in the Maelbeek metro station. A total of 32 people died and over 300 were injured. These attacks were also carried out by an IS cell. The Brussels attacks were further proof of the danger posed by IS cells in Europe. The attackers belonged to the same group responsible for the Paris attacks, highlighting the cross-border threat.

Nice, France (July 14, 2016) A man drove a truck into a crowd gathered for France's National Day, killing 86 people. The perpetrator had contacts with IS and was inspired by the group, although he was not directly connected to them. The Nice attack was one of the most devastating and revealed the increasing use of vehicles as weapons. He also showed the difficulty of identifying and stopping "lone wolves".

Berlin, Germany (19 December 2016) Attack on the Christmas market: A Tunisian asylum seeker with ties to ISIS hijacked a truck and drove into a Christmas market in central Berlin. He killed 12 people and injured 56 others. The IS claimed the attack. This attack showed the vulnerability of public places and led to increased security measures at Christmas markets and similar events across Europe.

Manchester, UK (22 May 2017) Suicide bombing after a concert: A suicide bomber detonated a bomb after an Ariana Grande concert at the Manchester Arena, killing 22 people, including many children, and injuring hundreds. IS claimed the attack. The Manchester attack showed ISIS's willingness to use particularly cruel tactics by targeting young people. It caused horror worldwide and led to intensive anti-terror measures in Great Britain.

Barcelona, Spain (August 17-18, 2017) Vehicle attack on Las Ramblas and Cambrils: A van crashed into a crowd of people on Barcelona's popular Las Ramblas promenade, killing 14 people. The following day, there was a similar attack in Cambrils, in which a woman was killed. The perpetrators were part of an IS cell. These attacks highlighted that Spain was also a target of ISIS and how the group expanded to various European countries. The events led to an intense debate about the security precautions in tourist hotspots.

London, United Kingdom (March 22, 2017, June 3, 2017, September 15, 2017) Three attacks in 2017:
On March 22, 2017, a man drove a car into a group of pedestrians on Westminster Bridge and then stabbed a police officer. Five people were killed.
On 3 June 2017, a van raced across London Bridge, and the occupants subsequently stabbed people in Borough Market, killing eight people.
On 15 September 2017, a bomb exploded on a London Underground train at Parsons Green station, injuring 30 people. The bomb detonated only partially.
The attacks in London showed that Britain remained a prime target of ISIS. They also highlighted the variety of tactics the group uses to maximize its acts of terrorism.

Strasbourg, France (11 December 2018) Attack on the Christmas market: A man opened fire on the Christmas market in Strasbourg, killing five people before being killed by the police. IS claimed the attack, although the perpetrator's connection to the group was unclear. The attack in Strasbourg once again showed the danger posed by "lone wolves" inspired by the ideology of ISIS. Christmas markets in Europe remain potential targets for terrorist attacks.

ISIS attacks in Europe follow certain patterns that provide valuable insights into the group's strategies and goals.

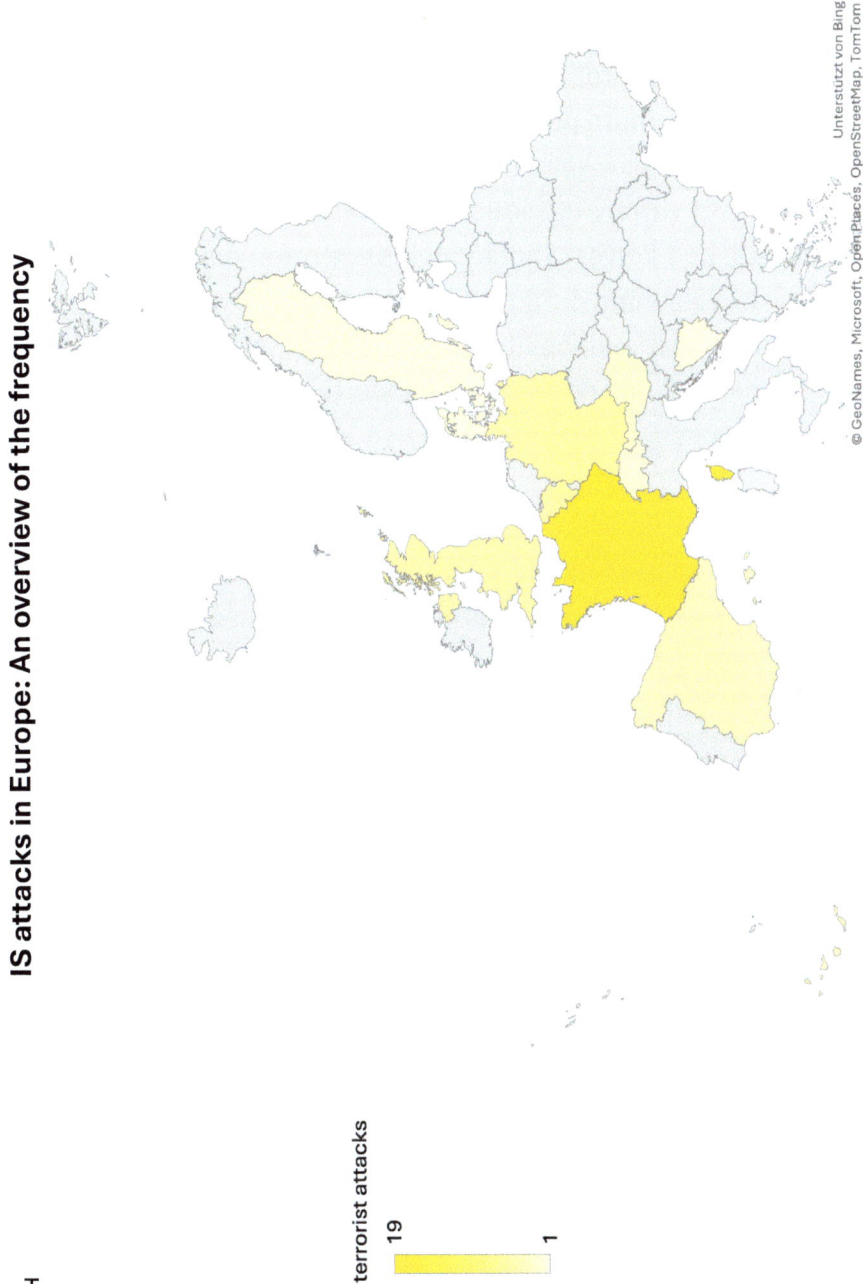

© GeoNames, Microsoft, Open Places, OpenStreetMap, TomTom

Unterstützt von Bing

terrorist attacks

19

1

The attacks are often concentrated in places with high symbolic value, such as religious sites, government buildings, and busy public squares. These targets are easily accessible and allow for maximum psychological damage.

ISIS uses a variety of tactics, including firearms, explosives, vehicles, and knives. These tactics are often easy to execute, which makes them particularly attractive to "lone wolves." The simplicity and availability of the means used also make it more difficult for security agencies to foresee and prevent such attacks.

Timing Coordination: Many of ISIS's attacks in Europe were carried out during major national or religious holidays, which maximized symbolic impact and increased media attention. Examples of this are the attack on the Christmas market in Berlin and the national holiday in Nice.

Collaborative cells and individual actors: While some attacks were carried out by well-organized cells with international ties, such as the attacks in Paris and Brussels, there were also numerous attacks carried out by individual actors. These "lone wolves" were often inspired and radicalized by ISIS propaganda on social media.

ISIS attacks have had a profound impact on Europe, both in terms of the security situation and the socio-political landscape. The attacks led to a tightening of security measures throughout Europe. Many countries increased surveillance of public places, strengthened border controls and intensified cooperation between security services at national and international level. The European Union introduced initiatives to combat radicalisation online and expanded resources to monitor terrorist activities.

One example of the tightened security situation is the establishment of anti-terror units that respond specifically to possible threats from IS. In France, for example, the state of emergency was extended several times after the attacks of 2015 and finally replaced by a permanent anti-terror law.

The IS attacks have led to increased Islamophobia and an upswing in right-wing extremist movements in Europe. The fear of further attacks and the increasing perception of Muslims as a potential threat have exacerbated the social climate in many European countries. This led to polarization, a rise in hate crimes, and an increase in populist political movements calling for tougher immigration policies and stricter security laws.

In countries such as France, Belgium and Germany, the IS attacks have sparked debates about the integration of migrants and the role of Islam in society. Some of these discussions have led to stricter immigration laws and increased surveillance of mosques and Islamic communities.

The attacks have also had economic consequences, especially in the tourism and retail sectors. Cities that were the target of attacks often saw a decline in tourist numbers and the associated loss of revenue. The attack on the Christmas market in Berlin, for example, led to a significant decline in the number of visitors to other Christmas markets in Germany and Europe.

The increased security measures have also led to rising public safety costs, as governments have had to invest more resources in counterterrorism measures and prevention.

The terrorist attacks of the Islamic State in Europe pose an ongoing and complex threat that goes far beyond the immediate physical damage. They have changed Europe's security architecture, exacerbated social tensions and triggered an ongoing debate about the balance between security and freedom.

The targeted choice of targets and the variety of tactics used illustrate the strategic planning behind the attacks and the continuing danger posed by radicalized lone perpetrators. Despite territorial losses in the Middle East, ISIS remains a serious threat to Europe due to its ideological presence and ability to inspire attacks.

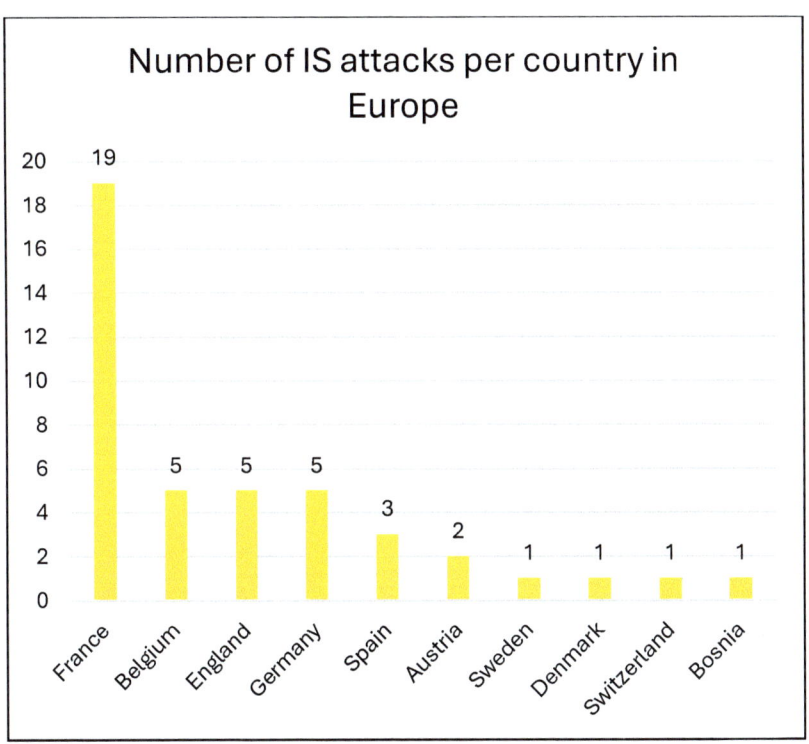

Number of IS attacks per country in Europe

France: 19
Belgium: 5
England: 5
Germany: 5
Spain: 3
Austria: 2
Sweden: 1
Denmark: 1
Switzerland: 1
Bosnia: 1

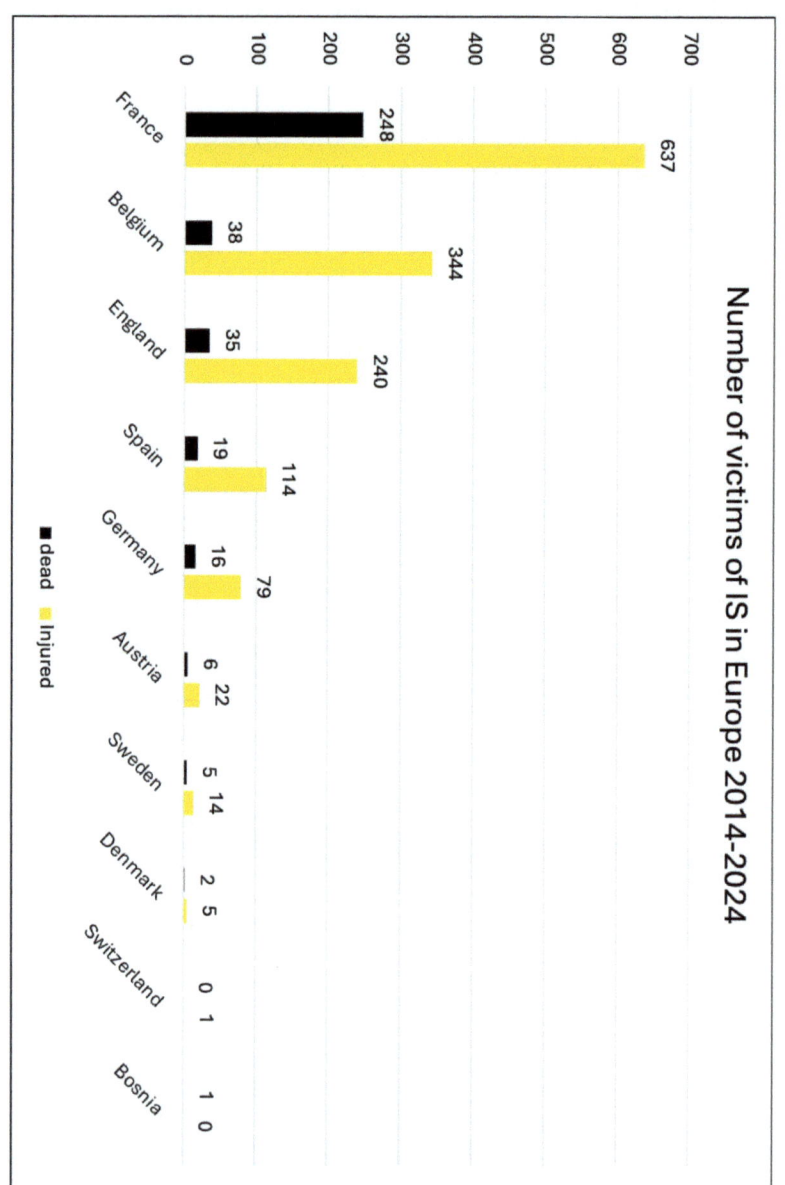

Number of victims of IS in Europe 2014-2024

- dead
- Injured

Country	dead	Injured
France	248	637
Belgium	38	344
England	35	240
Spain	19	114
Germany	16	79
Austria	6	22
Sweden	5	14
Denmark	2	5
Switzerland	0	1
Bosnia	1	0

THE LEGAL SYSTEM IN ISLAMIC STATES: SHARIA AND MODERN LEGISLATION

The legal system in Islamic states represents a complex inter-face between religious principles and modern legal frame-works. Islam, as one of the world's great monotheistic reli-gions, provides a comprehensive legal and moral guideline through Sharia (Islamic law) that extends to various aspects of life, including personal affairs, criminal law, business law, and international law. However, the application of Sharia varies greatly from state to state, depending on historical, cultural, and political contexts.

Sharia is a comprehensive religious legal system based on the teachings of the Qur'an and the Sunnah (the traditions of the Prophet Muhammad). It covers both religious command-ments and legal regulations and covers areas such as family law, inheritance law, criminal law, and contract law. Sharia aims to guide believers on the "right path" and to give them guidance on how to live a righteous and godly life.

Sharia is based on four main sources:
The Qur'an: The holy book of Islam, which is considered a di-rect revelation of God. It contains both specific legal provi-sions and general ethical guidelines.
The Sunnah: The traditions and actions of the Prophet Mu-hammad, which serve as a model for the behavior of believers.

The ijma': The consensus of Islamic scholars on certain legal issues, which is applied in cases where the Qur'an and the Sunnah do not provide clear answers.

The Qiyas: The analogical inferences, in which new legal questions are solved based on analogies to already decided cases in the Qur'an or the Sunnah.

Over the centuries, various schools of law (madhahib) developed in Islam, representing different interpretations of Sharia. The four main Sunni schools are the Hanafit, Maliki, Shafi'i and Hanbali schools of law. Each of these schools has its own methods of interpreting Sharia law and has different emphases in the application of the law.

Historically, Sharia was the dominant legal system in the Islamic empires, with the rulers (caliphs or sultans) ensuring the application of the laws. With the colonization of Islamic countries by European powers in the 19th and 20th centuries, many traditional legal systems were replaced or strongly influenced by Western-influenced codifications. After the independence of many Islamic states, the question arose as to the extent to which Sharia should be integrated into the modern state legal system.

In some Islamic states, such as Saudi Arabia and Iran, Sharia law forms the central foundation of the legal system. In Saudi Arabia, the entire legal system is based on the Hanbali interpretation of Sharia, with no written constitution or codified laws. In Iran, Sharia law forms the basis of the legal system, with the jurists (mujtahids) playing an important role in legislation and the interpretation of the laws.

In other Islamic states, there is a dual legal system in which Sharia law is applied alongside a modern, secular code of law. A prominent example of this is Egypt, where Sharia law prevails in certain areas such as family and inheritance law, while other areas such as criminal and civil law are largely governed by secular laws. In Pakistan, Sharia law is highly valued, but there are also modern laws based on British colonial law.

There are also Islamic states that are predominantly Muslim but have predominantly secular legal systems in which Sharia plays only a minor or symbolic role. In Turkey, which has established a secular system, Sharia law is not recognized as a source of legislation, although Islamic values echo in certain social and legal norms.

One of the biggest challenges in integrating Sharia law into modern legislative systems is the conflict with international human rights standards. There are considerable tensions, especially in the areas of women's rights, religious freedom and corporal punishment (such as flogging or amputation). Many Islamic states are under pressure to adapt their laws to international standards while remaining faithful to religious traditions.

In various Islamic states, there are efforts to reform Sharia law and adapt it to modern social and legal developments.

However, this often leads to tensions between traditionalists and reformers. The challenges are how to interpret and apply Sharia law in a way that both meets religious precepts and meets the requirements of a modern, pluralistic society.

Globalization and the influence of Western legal norms also have an impact on the legal systems in Islamic states. While some states are increasingly opening and modernizing their legislation, others see this as a threat to their religious identity and cultural heritage. The influence of international organizations and pressure from human rights groups also add to the complexity of legal developments in these countries.

The legal system in Islamic states is a dynamic and multi-layered field that is strongly influenced by Sharia law and its interpretation. While in some countries Sharia dominates the entire legal system, in others there are complex mixed systems in which both religious and secular laws coexist. The balance between preserving religious traditions and adapting to modern legal standards is one of the greatest challenges for Islamic states. Future developments will depend largely on how successfully these states manage to modernize their legal systems without losing their religious foundations and how they respond to demands for compliance with international human rights law.

IS AND THE FATE OF THE YAZIDIS: GENOCIDE AND ENSLAVEMENT

The genocide of the Yazidis by the Islamic State represents one of the darkest chapters in recent history. Since August 2014, IS has been committing systematic violent crimes against the Yazidi community in northern Iraq, which have been recognized as genocide by the international community. Thousands of Yazidis were killed, abducted or enslaved, while many women and children were victims of sexual violence.

The Yazidis are an ethnic-religious minority that lives mainly in northern Iraq, Syria and Turkey. Their religion, which combines elements of Zoroastrianism, Christianity and Islam, is monotheistic and worships the angel Melek Taus, the "peacock angel", as the central figure. Due to misunderstandings and prejudices—especially the misconception that the Yazidis worship Satan—they have been subjected to persecution throughout their history. These persecutions have shaped the Yazidi community and led it to organize itself into relatively closed communities to preserve its traditions and beliefs.

Before the rise of ISIS, the Yazidis lived mainly in the Sinjar region of northern Iraq, a strategically important but neglected and underdeveloped region. Although the Yazidis were a recognized minority in Iraq, they faced increasing discrimination and repression in the decades leading up to 2014, especially during the regime of Saddam Hussein. The political upheavals

153

following the US invasion in 2003 led to further destabilization of the region, leaving the Yazidi community increasingly isolated and vulnerable.

In the summer of 2014, IS launched a large-scale offensive in northern Iraq and overran the Sinjar region, home to most Yazidis. The Yazidi population was systematically attacked in the days and weeks that followed. Men and older boys were murdered, while women and children were abducted and enslaved. The offensive led to a humanitarian catastrophe as tens of thousands of Yazidis fled to the Sinjar mountains, where they were trapped without food, water or medical care.

IS committed systematic violent crimes against the Yazidi population, which were recognized as genocide by the international community. Thousands of Yazidi men were shot, beheaded or buried alive. Women and girls were considered "spoils of war" and sold in large numbers as sex slaves or "given away" to IS fighters. This practice was ideologically justified by an extremist interpretation of Islam, which attributed to the Yazidis the status of "infidels" who had no rights.
The crimes of sexual violence to which Yazidi women and girls were exposed were particularly serious. ISIS established a system of enslavement and forced marriage in which women were systematically raped, tortured and trafficked to other regions for "resale". This practice served not only to humiliate and control the Yazidi community, but also to recruit new fighters who were incentivized by the prospect of "spoils of war."

The international community initially reacted only hesitantly to the attacks of the IS on the Yazidis. It was only after the reports of the extent of the crimes and the humanitarian crisis in the Sinjar Mountains reached the world public that the US and its allies began targeted air strikes against IS positions in the region. This intervention helped to save the trapped people and slow down the advance of ISIS, but for many Yazidis, the help came too late.

In 2016, the U.S. State Department officially recognized ISIS's crimes against the Yazidis as genocide, an assessment that was later shared by the United Nations and several other states. This recognition was an important step towards recognizing the suffering of the Yazidi community and demanding justice. However, it also showed how difficult it is to reach an international agreement on the legal and moral assessment of such crimes.

Despite the recognition of the genocide, the international community faces significant challenges in prosecuting those responsible. While some IS members have been charged with war crimes and crimes against humanity in international courts or in their home countries, the comprehensive investigation of the crimes against the Yazidis remains difficult. Many perpetrators are still at large, and the evidence is extremely complex due to the uncertain situation in the region and the lack of forensic and documentary evidence.

The surviving Yazidis, especially the women and children, suffer from the psychological consequences of the violence they have suffered. Many of the survivors were raped, tortured and severely traumatized several times. Returning to a normal life is almost impossible for many, as psychological and social support in the affected regions is often inadequate. Long-term trauma management and psychological support are crucial to help survivors build a new life.

The genocide has deeply shaken the Yazidi community. Many of the surviving Yazidis are still living in refugee camps, their home villages and cities are in ruins. The reconstruction of the region and the return of the displaced is proving difficult as the security situation remains uncertain, and many Yazidis are unwilling to return to areas where they may feel threatened again. They also face the challenge of rebuilding their broken community, made more difficult by the loss of many members and the ongoing threat of discrimination and violence.

The genocide has destroyed not only physical lives, but also the cultural heritage of the Yazidis. Many holy sites and cultural artifacts were deliberately destroyed by IS to erase the identity of the Yazidis. The preservation and restoration of Yazidi culture, including its language, traditions and religious practices, are central to the survival of the community. This requires not only the reconstruction of physical structures, but also the promotion of education and the support of cultural initiatives.

The road to justice for the Yazidis is long and difficult. International efforts to prosecute those responsible are essential to bring justice to victims and prevent future crimes. Stronger international cooperation is needed to collect evidence, bring perpetrators to justice, and ensure that crimes against the Yazidis do not go unpunished.

Another important component of justice is the issue of compensation for the surviving Yazidis. This includes financial reparations as well as access to psychosocial support, medical care and education. Reparation payments could help give survivors a perspective for the future and support the reconstruction of the community. However, these efforts face major challenges, as many survivors still live in precarious conditions and the necessary resources are scarce.

Remembering the genocide and preserving collective memory are crucial to acknowledging the suffering of the Yazidis and preventing future crimes. Commemoration events, museums and educational programmed play an important role in raising awareness and creating a culture of remembrance. The international community has a responsibility to raise awareness of the crimes against the Yazidis and to ensure that these atrocities are not forgotten.

The genocide of the Yazidis by the Islamic State is one of the most serious crimes of the 21st century. The systematic murder, enslavement and rape of thousands of Yazidis shows the extreme effects of religious intolerance and extremist ideologies. The international community must learn from these events and ensure that such crimes are prevented in the future. This requires not only a determined prosecution of the perpetrators, but also comprehensive support for the surviving community to ensure its cultural and social survival. Only through a combination of legal reappraisal, cultural memory and international solidarity can it be ensured that the atrocities committed by IS do not go unpunished and that the Yazidis are given the opportunity to rebuild their community and live in peace.

A mass grave in the Sinjar region from 2015 that contains the remains of several dozen Yazidis buried after a massacre. Visible are bones of the victims protruding from the grave.

THE ROLE OF REGIONAL POWERS IN THE FIGHT AGAINST IS

The rise and expansion of the Islamic State (IS) in the Middle East has triggered a profound geopolitical crisis that extends far beyond the borders of Syria and Iraq. The fight against ISIS was not only a matter of international coalitions led by Western powers, but also a matter of regional security and stability. The regional powers – including Iran, Saudi Arabia, Turkey, Jordan and the Gulf states – played a crucial role in this conflict. Each of these powers had its own interests and strategies, which both influenced the course of the fight against IS and permanently changed the political landscape of the region.

Iran: Protecting power of the Shiite axis and opponent of IS

Iran played a key role in the fight against ISIS, especially in Syria and Iraq. As the dominant Shiite power in the region, Tehran saw ISIS not only as a threat to the stability of the region, but also as a direct enemy of its regional interests and allies.

Support for Shiite militias and the Iraqi government

In Iraq, Iran has been a major supporter of the Shiite government in Baghdad and its allied militias, collectively known as the Popular Mobilization Forces (PMF). These militias, often trained and armed directly by Iran, played a crucial role in the reconquest of territories occupied by ISIS. Iranian support was not only material, but also strategic. Senior Iranian military advisers, including the late General Qasem Soleimani, were directly involved in the operations against ISIS. This close co-operation strengthened Iranian influence in Iraq, but was also met with criticism and concern, especially from Sunni actors and Western states, who were skeptical of Tehran's growing influence.

Intervention in Syria in support of the Assad regime

In Syria, Iran was a key supporter of the regime of Bashar al-Assad, which was threatened by ISIS and other opposition groups. Tehran not only provided logistical and financial support, but also sent militias, especially the Lebanese Hezbollah, as well as its own Revolutionary Guards to strengthen the Syrian military. The Iranian intervention in Syria was aimed at keeping a loyal ally in power and securing the "Shiite axis" that stretches from Iran to Lebanon through Iraq and Syria. This strategy placed Iran in direct opposition to the Sunni regional powers and increased sectarian tensions in the region.

Saudi Arabia: Sunni leader and opponent of Iran's sphere of influence

Saudi Arabia, as one of the leading Sunni powers and a long-time rival of Iran, also had a strong interest in fighting ISIS, although its role in the fight against ISIS was marked by contradictions and complex geopolitical interests.

Support for the Syrian opposition and indirect confrontation with ISIS

In the Syrian civil war, Saudi Arabia supported various rebel groups that fought against the Assad regime. However, many of these groups were in competition with ISIS, which led to an indirect confrontation with the jihadist organization. Saudi Arabia tried to strike a balance between supporting the Sunni opposition and fighting ISIS, as the kingdom viewed ISIS's growing influence as a threat to its own stability and regional leadership.

Anti-IS coalition and Saudi military action
Saudi Arabia joined the US-led international coalition against ISIS and participated in airstrikes on ISIS positions in Syria and Iraq. However, this participation was limited and reflected the Kingdom's complex strategic priorities. While ISIS posed an immediate threat, Saudi Arabia focused more on the conflict in Yemen and containing Iranian influence in the region.

Turkey: An actor caught between the fronts
Turkey's role in the fight against IS was marked by ambivalence and a multitude of contradictory interests. As a NATO member and an important regional player, Turkey pursued its own agenda, which often contradicted the goals of other coalition participants.

Border security and the fight against IS
Turkey has long been an important access point for foreign fighters who wanted to join ISIS in Syria. Although the Turkish government officially classified ISIS as a terrorist organization, it was accused of not doing enough to stop the influx of fighters. It was only when IS increasingly became a threat to

Turkey's internal security, especially through attacks on Turkish soil, that Ankara intensified its measures against the group.

Conflict with the Kurds and strategic priorities

Another factor that influenced Turkey's attitude towards ISIS was the conflict with the Kurdish PKK and its Syrian offshoots, the People's Protection Units (YPG). Turkey considers the YPG a terrorist organization, while it played a key role in the international coalition in the fight against IS. This conflict of interest led to tensions within the coalition and Turkish military interventions in northern Syria, which were officially directed against ISIS, but were primarily aimed at preventing the spread of Kurdish power.

Jordan and the Gulf States: Regional Stability and Contribution to the International Coalition

Jordan and the Gulf States, especially Qatar, the United Arab Emirates and Kuwait, also played important roles in the fight against ISIS, albeit in different ways and with different priorities.

Jordan: Frontline state in the fight against IS

Jordan, which borders directly on Syria and Iraq, was severely affected by the threat of IS from the beginning. The country was home to many Syrian refugees and was the target of ISIS attacks and infiltration attempts. As part of the international coalition, Jordan participated in airstrikes against ISIS and strengthened its border security to prevent the conflict from spilling over into its territory. Jordan's role was crucial, as the country acted as a buffer zone between the unstable neighboring states and the Gulf states.

The role of the Gulf States

The Gulf States, notably Qatar and the United Arab Emirates, also participated in the international coalition against ISIS, mainly through financial and logistical support, as well as participation in airstrikes. Their main concern was stability in the region and the containment of the jihadist threat, which emanated not only from ISIS, but also from other radical groups. However, there were also tensions and differences among the Gulf states themselves, especially regarding support for various Islamist groups in Syria.

Qatar and its complex role in regional politics

Qatar, which is known for its support of Islamist movements, has often been viewed critically for its role in the Syrian civil war and the fight against IS. While Qatar was part of the coalition against IS, the emirate was accused of also supporting groups that were ideologically close to IS. These contradictory actions reflected Qatar's efforts to secure and expand its influence in the region, but this led to tensions with neighbors, especially Saudi Arabia and the United Arab Emirates.

Effects and long-term consequences

The interventions of the regional powers in the fight against ISIS have had a profound impact on the geopolitical landscape of the Middle East. While ISIS has been largely defeated as a territorial actor, the divisions and rivalries that have been exacerbated by the conflict persist and continue to shape the dynamics in the region.

The fight against IS increased the already existing sectarian tensions between Sunnis and Shiites in the region. Iran and its allies have been able to significantly expand their influence in Syria and Iraq, leading to increased rivalry with Saudi Arabia and other Sunni states. These tensions continue to contribute to instability in the region and make it difficult to find a political solution to the ongoing conflicts.

The military successes of Iranian-backed forces, especially in Syria, led to a shift in the regional balance of power in favor of Tehran. This development has not only redefined relations between regional powers but has also influenced the intervention of external actors such as Russia and the US, each of which has its own interests in the region.

Despite the military success against ISIS, many of the underlying problems that led to its rise remain unresolved. The continued instability in Syria, Iraq and the sectarian division of the region continue to provide fertile ground for extremist ideologies and could create new threats in the future. The role of regional powers will be decisive in whether these challenges are addressed through cooperation and dialogue or through ongoing rivalries and conflicts.

THE U.S. ROLE IN THE MIDDLE EAST: INFLUENCE ON THE ISLAMIC STATE

The role of the United States in the Middle East has shaped the political and security landscape of the region for decades. Over the past two decades, US policy has increasingly focused on combating terrorism and the Islamic State (IS) in particular. The rise of ISIS after the Iraq war in 2003 and during the Syrian civil war from 2011 onwards was one of the greatest challenges for US foreign policy.

U.S. influence in the Middle East dates to the mid-20th century, but the events that followed the September 11, 2001, attacks marked a turning point in American policy in the region. The invasion of Iraq in 2003 was a decisive factor in the subsequent developments that led to the rise of ISIS.

The US invasion of Iraq in 2003, which ended with the overthrow of Saddam Hussein, had a profound impact on the stability of the country and the entire region. The US-led coalition aimed to establish a stable, democratic government in Iraq, but the dissolution of the Iraqi army and the removal of the Baath Party from power led to a power vacuum and increased sectarian tensions between Sunnis and Shiites. Out of this chaos, various Sunni insurgent groups formed that would later become the core of the Islamic State in Iraq.

The fight against IS became a central goal of US policy in the Middle East from 2014 onwards. The American strategy included a combination of military operations, support for regional partners, and international diplomatic efforts.

The central US military operation against IS was Operation Inherent Resolve, launched in 2014. This multinational operation aimed to fight ISIS in Syria and Iraq through airstrikes, support for local ground troops and special operations. The U.S. led the international coalition, which consisted of more than 70 countries, and played a leading role in coordinating military efforts. Through targeted air strikes, the support of the Iraqi army and Kurdish forces (Peshmerga) and the Syrian Democratic Forces (SDF), it was possible to gradually drive IS out of its occupied territories.

An essential part of the US strategy was the support of regional partners. In Iraq, the U.S. focused on training and equipping Iraqi security forces, which were significantly weakened after the withdrawal of U.S. troops in 2011. This support was crucial for the reconquest of cities like Mosul. In Syria, the US worked closely with the Kurdish-led SDF, which was considered one of the most effective forces against IS. However, this partnership was complex and led to tensions with Turkey, which the SDF sees as allied with the PKK, an organization designated by Ankara as a terrorist organization.

In addition to military measures, the US relied on diplomatic efforts to forge a broad international coalition against IS. This coalition included not only military contributions, but also financial and humanitarian support. The U.S. played a central role in coordinating these efforts, striving to reconcile the different interests and priorities of the countries involved. In addition, the US urged its partners to take measures to curb the financing of ISIS, especially through the illegal oil trade.

The U.S.-led strategy was successful in many ways, but it also had unexpected consequences that reflect the complex nature of the conflict in the Middle East.

Thanks to intensive military operations and cooperation with local ground troops, IS was largely driven out of its territorial strongholds in Syria and Iraq by 2019. The recapture of Mosul in Iraq and Raqqa in Syria, the two most important cities of ISIS, marked the end of the caliphate in its territorial form. These military successes led to a significant weakening of ISIS's operational capabilities and its ability to plan and carry out large-scale attacks

The war against ISIS has had significant humanitarian consequences, especially in the areas controlled by ISIS. The intense bombings and ground offensives led to massive destruction and civilian casualties. Millions of people have been displaced, and the affected societies have been traumatized. The US and its partners also had to deal with the long-term challenges of rebuilding and stabilizing the liberated areas in order to prevent a resurgence of ISIS. This included the restoration of basic services, the promotion of reconciliation processes and the support of local governance structures.

U.S. policy in the Middle East, especially in the context of ISIS, has been fraught with numerous challenges and controversies. These affected both the domestic political debate in the US and relations with regional and global partners.

U.S. cooperation with Kurdish forces in Syria led to significant tensions with Turkey, a key NATO ally. Ankara viewed the Kurdish YPG units, which formed the core of the SDF, as a threat to its own national security. These tensions escalated in 2019 when the US, under the administration of Donald Trump, announced the withdrawal of its troops from northern Syria, thus enabling a Turkish military offensive against the Kurds. This decision was heavily criticized both internationally and within the US, as it was perceived as a betrayal of an important ally in the fight against ISIS.

The continued US presence and military operations in the Middle East led to an intense domestic debate about the long-term role of the US in the region. While some argued that the US should reduce its presence and focus on competing with major powers such as China and Russia, others warned of the risks of a premature withdrawal that could allow a resurgence of ISIS or other extremist groups. This debate was reflected in the different approaches of successive US administrations, from Barack Obama to Donald Trump to Joe Biden.

The US strategy in the fight against IS has also had an impact on relations with other regional powers, including Iran and Saudi Arabia. While Iran and its allies in Syria and Iraq have also fought ISIS, they have often been in competition with US-backed forces. This led to a complex interaction between cooperation and confrontation in different parts of the region. Saudi Arabia, on the other hand, largely supported US policy, but had its own concerns about Iran's role and the spread of its influence after the defeat of ISIS.

The fight against ISIS has dominated US policy in the Middle East in recent years and will continue to influence regional and global developments.
Although ISIS has been largely defeated as a territorial power, it remains an ongoing threat, both in the region and globally. ISIS's ability to adapt to changing circumstances and spread its ideology globally poses a challenge to long-term stability. The U.S. and its international partners face the task of addressing not only the military aspects of counterterrorism, but also the underlying political, economic, and social causes that lead to radicalization.

The experiences in the fight against IS have had a lasting impact on US foreign policy in the Middle East. Debates about the right balance between military engagement and diplomatic restraint will continue to influence U.S. strategy in the region. In addition, the lessons learned from the fight against ISIS may shape future U.S. policy in other conflict zones around the world, especially with regard to countering non-state actors and transnational threats.

The challenges of reconstruction and political stabilisation in the areas liberated from IS are enormous. The U.S. plays an important role in international reconstruction efforts, but the success of these efforts depends on cooperation with regional actors and the international community. The long-term stability of the Middle East will depend crucially on its ability to address the root causes of violence and extremism and to find sustainable political solutions to the region's deep-rooted conflicts.

The role of the US in the Middle East and its influence on the Islamic State are closely linked. While the military successes of the US and its partners have led to the dismantling of the IS caliphate, the long-term challenges for the region and the world remain. The fight against ISIS has not only influenced regional geopolitics, but also shaped the direction of US foreign policy and the global security architecture. The future of the Middle East will depend largely on how the United States and its partners address the complex political, social, and economic challenges that continue to destabilize the region and feed extremism.

RUSSIA'S INVOLVEMENT IN SYRIA AND THE INFLUENCE ON IS

Since the beginning of the Syrian civil war in 2011, Russia has positioned itself as one of the central players in this complex conflict. Russia's involvement in Syria marked a turning point in the international dynamics of the Middle East and had a significant impact on the regional security situation, including the fight against the Islamic State (IS). While Moscow's official discourse spoke of the need to fight global terrorism, including ISIS, Russia pursued a multi-layered strategy in Syria that pursued both geopolitical and military goals.

Russia's engagement in Syria is deeply rooted in historical, geopolitical and security considerations. Relations between Moscow and Damascus date back to Soviet times, when Syria was one of the USSR's closest allies in the Middle East. These relations were largely maintained after the collapse of the Soviet Union and played a crucial role in Moscow's decision to support the Assad regime.

A central motive for Russia's involvement in Syria was the goal of consolidating its influence in the Middle East and being perceived as a global player on an equal footing with the US and its allies. Syria offered Moscow the opportunity to maintain its only Mediterranean base in Tartus and expand its military presence in the region. In addition, Russia saw the Syrian conflict as an opportunity to defend the principle of national sovereignty against Western intervention and to prevent precedents for regime change through external pressure.

From the very beginning, it was clear that Russia stood firmly by the side of Syrian President Bashar al-Assad. Moscow viewed Assad as a stable and reliable partner whose overthrow would lead to chaos and potentially strengthen extremist forces, including ISIS. Russia argued that a collapse of the Assad regime could destabilize the entire Middle East and further fuel terrorism.

On September 30, 2015, Russia officially began a full-scale military intervention in Syria. This decision marked an escalation of the conflict and was a decisive factor during the war.

The Russian government justified its intervention in Syria by citing the need to fight international terrorism, especially ISIS. In Moscow's official account, it was a preventive measure to prevent terrorism from advancing further into Russia and its spheres of influence. In fact, thousands of fighters from the North Caucasus and Central Asia had joined ISIS, posing a real threat to Russia.

Although the Russian airstrikes were officially directed against ISIS, they were often directed against a wide range of opposition groups, including those supported by the US and other Western states. Much of the Russian airstrikes were concentrated in areas controlled by other rebel groups, especially near strategically important cities such as Aleppo and Idlib. IS was also a target of Russian attacks, but not the main target. This tactic was aimed at weakening opposition to Assad and consolidating his position.

Russia's military involvement in Syria was not in isolation, but in close coordination with Iran and the Lebanese Hezbollah, which also supported Assad. This cooperation allowed Russia to maximize its military successes and complement logistics and the deployment of ground troops. At the diplomatic level, Russia also cooperated with Turkey, despite tensions caused by the shooting down of a Russian fighter jet by the Turkish Air Force in November 2015. This cooperation was later institutionalized by the Astana peace talks, in which Russia, Turkey and Iran tried to find a solution to the Syrian conflict. Russia's military intervention in Syria has had a significant impact on the dynamics of the conflict and thus also on ISIS.

Russia's airstrikes and support for the Syrian army contributed to the recapture of several areas previously controlled by ISIS, including the historic city of Palmyra, which was liberated in March 2016. These successes were celebrated in the Russian media as proof of the effectiveness of Russia's military strategy and contribution to the global fight against terrorism.

At the same time, the Russian attacks on other opposition groups had unintended consequences. By weakening the moderate opposition and other rebel groups, IS has been able to strengthen its position in certain areas or at least benefit from the destabilization of its opponents. This dynamic showed the complex interactions within the Syrian war zone, where different actors fought for supremacy.

Russia also used its fight against ISIS as part of a broader propaganda campaign to showcase its role as a responsible global actor and a bulwark against terrorism. This was supported by intense media coverage that highlighted Russian military successes while portraying Western efforts as ineffective. This propaganda was not only aimed at the international community, but also served to legitimize the Russian government domestically and mobilize public support for military engagement.

Russia's involvement in Syria has had a decisive influence not only on the course of the Syrian civil war, but also on far-reaching geopolitical consequences that go beyond the immediate conflict.

Russia's intervention in Syria has strengthened Moscow's position as a central power in the Middle East. By supporting the Assad regime, Russia has not only expanded its military presence in the region but has also established itself as an indispensable player in regional diplomacy. This was evident in the numerous peace negotiations in which Russia played a key role.

The Russian intervention in Syria led to an intensification of tensions between Russia and Western states, especially the United States. While both sides officially supported the fight against ISIS, there were significant differences of opinion about the tactics and goals of each engagement. These tensions were also reflected in NATO, where member states debated how to deal with Russia's actions.

Despite the military successes, Syria's long-term stability remains uncertain. Russia's support for Assad has strengthened the regime, but it has also left the country's fundamental political and social problems unresolved. These challenges, including ongoing sectarian tensions and the reconstruction of the devastated country, could provoke new conflicts in the future and possibly the resurgence of extremist groups such as ISIS.

With Assad's military victory and the widespread defeat of ISIS, Russia also turned its attention to the economic reconstruction of Syria, which offered Moscow further opportunities to consolidate its influence in the region.

Russia is interested in benefiting from the reconstruction of Syria, especially through contracts in the energy and construction sectors. These economic activities allow Russia to secure its presence in Syria in the long term while reaping economic benefits from its support for Assad.

Despite these ambitions, Russia faces significant challenges in rebuilding Syria, particularly due to international sanctions and limited support from Western states. Cooperation with other regional actors, including Iran and Turkey, will be crucial to ensure the stability of the country and finally cut off the influence of ISIS and other extremist groups.

OPERATION INHERENT RESOLVE

Operation Inherent Resolve is the code name for the international military campaign launched in 2014 by the United States and a coalition of partners to stop and roll back the advance of the Islamic State (IS) in Iraq and Syria. This operation marks a significant moment in modern military history, as it aimed both to recapture large areas and to dismantle ISIS's territorial base. The complexity of this campaign, the multiplicity of actors involved, and the long-term strategic implications make Operation Inherent Resolve a central topic in the discussion of international security and counterterrorism.

The United States, which had been militarily engaged in Iraq since the fall of Saddam Hussein in 2003, was forced to intervene again militarily because of the rapid advance of ISIS and the humanitarian catastrophes it unleashed. The decision to launch Operation Inherent Resolve was made against the backdrop of a broad international coalition that came together to fight ISIS. This coalition included both Western states and regional powers from the Middle East. In August 2014, President Barack Obama approved the first air strikes against IS positions in Iraq.

The main goal of Operation Inherent Resolve was the "degradation and eventual destruction" of the Islamic State. This goal was to be achieved through a combination of airstrikes, support for local ground troops and the dismantling of ISIS's financial and recruitment networks. The operation was aimed at curbing the territorial expansion of ISIS, destroying critical infrastructure and liberating the areas controlled by the extremists.

Operation Inherent Resolve was designed from the beginning as a multinational effort. The coalition included over 70 states and organizations that contributed to the success of the mission in various ways. While the U.S. carried out most of the airstrikes, other NATO countries and regional partners provided reconnaissance support, logistical assistance, and humanitarian assistance. Countries such as France, Britain and Australia also carried out airstrikes, while partners such as Jordan and the United Arab Emirates focused on countering ISIS propaganda and funding.

A central aspect of OIR's strategy was to support local forces acting as "proxies" on the ground. In Iraq, the coalition supported the Iraqi army, the Kurdish Peshmerga and various militias in the fight against IS. In Syria, the Syrian Democratic Alliance (SDF), which was predominantly led by Kurdish fighters, became the main ground force against IS. This strategy was designed to minimize the risk to Western troops by relying on local forces equipped with air support and arms supplies.

In the first months after the start of the operation, the airstrikes focused on containing the IS advance and protecting critical infrastructure and the civilian population. The attacks targeted IS fighters, weapons depots, oil fields and logistical facilities. This phase of the operation was crucial to break the momentum of ISIS and prevent the advance in Baghdad. At the same time, the coalition began to equip and train the Iraqi and Kurdish forces to create the conditions for a counteroffensive.

The battle for Mosul, which began in October 2016 and ended in July 2017 with the recapture of the city, marked a turning point in the fight against ISIS. Mosul was the largest city under ISIS control and had symbolic significance as the site of al-Baghdadi's proclamation of the caliphate. The recapture of Mosul was the result of intense fighting in which

Iraqi troops, Kurdish Peshmerga and the coalition worked closely together.

At the same time, SDF troops in Syria began the siege of Raqqa, the unofficial capital of IS. The battle for Raqqa, which began in June 2017 and ended in October 2017, led to the destruction of ISIS's administrative and military center in Syria. The recapture of Raqqa was another significant success for the coalition, but it also led to significant destruction and civilian casualties.

Although IS largely lost its territorial base after the losses of Mosul and Raqqa, it was not completely defeated. Many fighters retreated to rural areas or the desert, from where they carried out guerrilla tactics against the coalition and local forces. In addition, IS increasingly shifted to terrorist attacks outside its original sphere of influence, especially in Europe and other parts of the world. This showed that despite its defeats, the organization continued to pose a threat and was able to adapt quickly to changing circumstances.

OIR's military operations have had massive humanitarian consequences. Cities such as Mosul and Raqqa were severely damaged by the fighting, and there were great civilian casualties. It is estimated that thousands of civilians died in the airstrikes and ground fighting, and millions were displaced. The humanitarian crisis in the region continued to worsen as the reconstruction of infrastructure, health services and housing progressed slowly.

After the military victory over ISIS, Iraq and Syria faced the enormous challenge of restoring political stability and functioning government structures. In Iraq, deep ethnic and religious tensions between Shiites, Sunnis and Kurds hampered reconstruction and national reconciliation. In Syria, the political situation remained unstable due to the ongoing civil war and rival regional and international interests. The lack of political progress and ongoing uncertainty increased the risk that radical groups could regain a foothold.

Operation Inherent Resolve also had far-reaching implications for global security. ISIS used its media literacy and widespread use of social media to create an international network of followers who carried out attacks in their home countries. The return of foreign fighters to their home countries posed an additional security threat, as these experienced and radicalized fighters are difficult to monitor and rehabilitate. Combating this transnational threat remains one of the greatest challenges facing the international community.

Despite the successes of Operation Inherent Resolve, ISIS remains active, albeit in a different form. The organization has decentralized and now operates as a network of cells and followers in various regions, particularly in Africa and Southeast Asia. Countering this new form of ISIS requires adapted strategies that focus not only on military action, but also on combating the ideological foundations of extremism and strengthening local governance structures.

Operation Inherent Resolve has shown that multinational cooperation is crucial in the fight against terrorism. Coordination between various military, intelligence and diplomatic actors contributed significantly to the success of the operation. Future counterterrorism strategies must continue to rely on this international cooperation to be able to react flexibly to new threats. At the same time, the case of OIR shows the limits of military interventions, especially about the sustainable reconstruction and political stabilization of crisis regions.

The operation has also sparked a discussion about respect for human rights and accountability in military campaigns. The reports of civilian casualties and the destruction of infrastructure in the affected areas have highlighted the need to comply with strict rules for military operations in densely populated areas. The responsibility of the international community not only to achieve short-term military victories, but also to create stable and just conditions in the long term, is one of the central lessons of Operation Inherent Resolve.

Operation Inherent Resolve was one of the most significant military interventions of recent decades, which in many ways redefined the modern fight against transnational terrorism. The operation was successful in destroying the territorial caliphate of the Islamic State and breaking its military strength. However, the continuing threat posed by IS in its new form, as well as the profound political and humanitarian challenges in the affected regions, show that the fight against extremist groups such as IS goes far beyond military victory. Long-term stability and security can only be achieved through a combination of military, political, diplomatic, and humanitarian measures that both address the immediate threats and address the root causes of extremism.

THE DECLINE OF THE CALIPHATE IN THE ISLAMIC STATE: LOSS OF TERRITORIES AND LEADERS

The territorial disintegration of the caliphate began in earnest in 2015, when an international coalition led by the United States began to carry out airstrikes on ISIS positions. These airstrikes, together with ground offensives by Kurdish, Iraqi and Syrian forces, led to a gradual withdrawal of ISIS from its main strongholds.

Battle of Kobane (2014-2015): One of the first symbolic losses for IS was the battle for the Syrian city of Kobane. The Kurdish People's Protection Units (YPG), supported by US air strikes, were able to recapture the city after months of fighting. The loss of Kobane marked a turning point in the fight against ISIS, as it showed that the group was not invincible.

Recapture of Ramadi and Fallujah (2016): In Iraq, Iraqi forces, supported by the international coalition, conducted successful operations to recapture the cities of Ramadi and Fallujah. These cities were important strategic centers for ISIS in western Iraq, and their loss greatly weakened the group's logistics and moral base.

Battle of Mosul (2016-2017): The recapture of Mosul was a decisive blow against ISIS. The Battle of Mosul lasted almost nine months and was marked by fierce fighting. The loss of Mosul meant the end of IS as a territorial power factor in Iraq.

Raqqa (2017): The Syrian city of Raqqa was considered the unofficial capital of the caliphate and was a central symbol of ISIS's power. In October 2017, Raqqa was recaptured by the Syrian Democratic Forces (SDF), supported by the international coalition. The fall of Raqqa sealed the territorial collapse of IS in Syria.

The loss of territory was particularly devastating for ISIS, as its legitimacy and appeal were strongly linked to the idea of the caliphate. ISIS propaganda repeatedly emphasized the need to control and defend Islamic territory. With the loss of these territories, IS lost not only important resources, but also a large part of its ideological credibility. The territorial defeats also led to a decline in recruitment numbers, as many foreign fighters abandoned their travel plans to the Middle East or deserted.

ISIS was highly centralized and highly dependent on the leadership of charismatic and strategically savvy personalities. These leaders were crucial to ISIS's ideology, organization, and operational capability. The loss of these key people contributed significantly to the weakening of the organization.

In the course of the military operations against IS, numerous high-ranking leaders were deliberately killed. These targeted killings were carried out primarily through drone strikes and special operations by the US-led coalition.

Abu Bakr al-Baghdadi: The self-proclaimed caliph and leader of ISIS, Abu Bakr al-Baghdadi, was the face of the organization and a central figure in its ideological orientation. He was killed in October 2019 during a US special operation in the Syrian province of Idlib. The death of al-Baghdadi left a power vacuum and led to an internal crisis within ISIS, as his succession was unclear, and the organization lost cohesion.

Abu Muhammad al-Adnani: Al-Adnani was the official spokesman for ISIS and one of the main architects of the group's international terror strategy. He played a crucial role in coordinating attacks abroad, including the attacks in Paris in 2015. Al-Adnani was killed in an airstrike in August 2016, which significantly weakened ISIS's ability to plan and conduct global operations.

Abu Omar al-Shishani: Known as "the Chechen," al-Shishani was a high-ranking military commander of ISIS and a key figure in military operations in Syria. He was killed in a US air strike in July 2016. Al-Shishani's death was a major blow to ISIS's military leadership, as he was considered one of the group's most capable and experienced commanders.

Abu Bakr al-Baghdadi's successor: After the death of al-Baghdadi, IS appointed Abu Ibrahim al-Hashimi al-Qurayshi as its new leader. However, al-Qurayshi was also killed in a US special operation in February 2022, further exacerbating ISIS's leadership crisis.

The loss of leaders had a profound impact on ISIS's organization and coherence. These killings destabilized the central leadership and led to power struggles and internal tensions. In addition, they complicated ISIS's ability to coordinate large-scale operations and maintain its propaganda at the same level as before. The targeted elimination of key personnel undermined ISIS's organizational efficiency and reduced its attractiveness to new recruits, who were deterred by increasing instability.

In addition to the loss of territories and leaders, internal factors also contributed to the decline of the caliphate. From the beginning, ISIS was a highly centralized organization based on the personal networks and ideological vision of al-Baghdadi and his inner circle. This centralization led to a dependence on a few key people and made the organization vulnerable to targeted killings.

In addition, the brutal and repressive rule of IS led to increasing alienation of the population in the areas under its control. The draconian punishments and extreme interpretation of Sharia law enforced by ISIS led to resistance and uprisings that further undermined the stability of the caliphate.

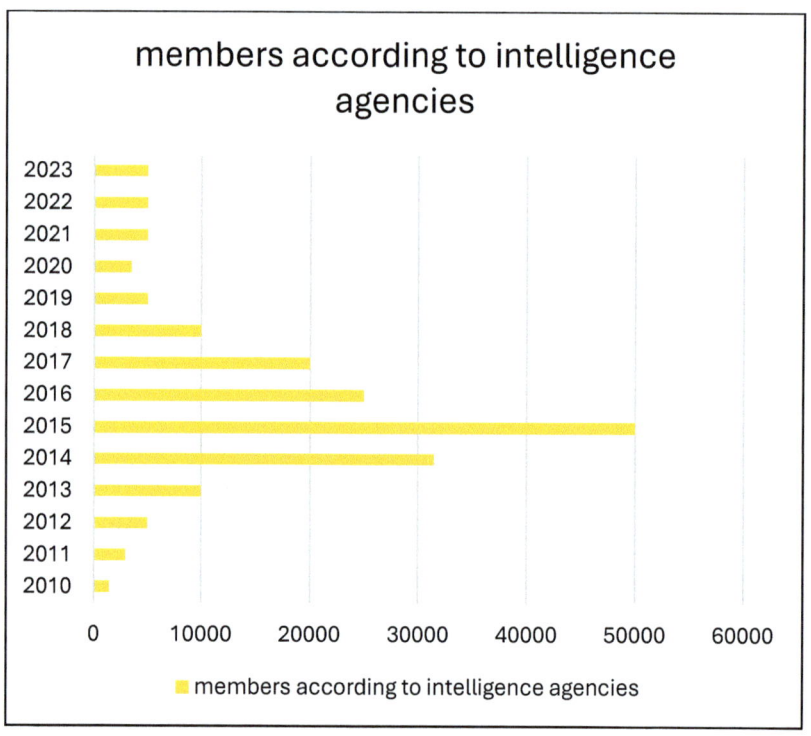

The available data shows the estimated number of members of the Islamic State (IS) according to intelligence agencies from 2010 to 2023. In the first few years, from 2010 to 2012, the number of members was low, starting with about 1,500 members in 2010 and rising to 5,000 by 2012.

A marked increase was recorded in 2013, when the number of members grew to 10,000. The largest increase took place in 2014, when the number of members rose to 31,500. This correlates with ISIS's intensive military expansion and territorial control in Iraq and Syria.

In 2015, IS reached its peak with about 50,000 members. After that, however, membership began to decline, indicating military defeats and geopolitical changes in the region. In 2016, the number was still high at 25,000 members but fell to 5,000 by 2019. In the following years, the number fluctuated between 3,500 and 5,000, indicating a stabilization of the remaining members, despite ongoing military efforts against the group.

THE ISLAMIC STATE AFTER THE CALIPHATE: FRAGMENTATION AND REALIGNMENT

After the loss of its caliphate, ISIS disintegrated into different, loosely connected groups operating in different regions of the world. This fragmentation is a characteristic feature of ISIS in the post-Caliphate era.

Regional offshoots and affiliate groups

With the territorial collapse in Syria and Iraq, ISIS increasingly shifted its activities to other regions, especially Africa, South Asia and Central Asia. This realignment was reflected in the increased activity of IS offshoots such as Khorasan Province in Afghanistan, West Africa Province (ISWAP) in Nigeria and Sinai Province in Egypt.

These groups operate largely independently of each other but share an ideological orientation and commitment to the global jihadist movement. They operate in local conflicts and use regional instabilities to consolidate their positions. Through this fragmentation, ISIS has expanded its geographical reach and developed a flexible structure that is harder to fight than a centralized caliphate.

Fragmentation was accompanied by a decentralization of leadership. After the death of the first IS caliph Abu Bakr al-Baghdadi in October 2019, Abu Ibrahim al-Hashimi al-Qurayshi took over the leadership. But he was also killed in February

2022. Leadership positions have been refilled several times since then, indicating the challenges the organization faces in terms of leadership and coherence.

However, decentralization also allowed ISIS to develop greater resilience to military pressure. Instead of relying on a central leadership that could be eliminated by targeted attacks, the various groups operate autonomously and are therefore less susceptible to complete dismantling.

The realignment of IS after the loss of its caliphate included both strategic and tactical adjustments. These changes were crucial to the organization's survival in a world where it no longer has a fixed territory.

One of the most important strategic adjustments of the IS was the return to a classic insurgency strategy. IS had already successfully used this strategy before the proclamation of the caliphate in 2014. After losing its territory, ISIS returned to this tactic by conducting guerrilla operations, planning and executing attacks, and supporting local insurgencies. This allowed ISIS to continue to be present as a threat in the affected regions without having to focus on defending territory.

Another central aspect of ISIS's realignment was the increased use of propaganda and digital networks. Even after the loss of its caliphate, IS remained able to spread its messages via the Internet and social media. This propaganda served not only to recruit new followers, but also to maintain moral and ideological coherence among the remaining fighters and supporters.

The IS propaganda machine has proven to be remarkably resilient despite military defeats. It has helped keep the myth of ISIS alive and mobilize its global following, especially in regions where the group is still active.

Another important adaptation of ISIS was its ability to adapt to local conditions. In regions such as the Sahel in Africa, where state structures are weak and ethnic tensions exist, IS has formed alliances with local groups and exploited existing conflicts to expand its influence. This adaptability has even allowed ISIS to gain influence in some regions, although the organization has been weakened on a global scale.

WHO BECOMES A TERRORIST?

The question of who becomes IS terrorists in Europe requires a differentiated analysis that takes into account a variety of social, political, psychological and cultural factors. This analysis examines the recruitment processes, the socio-demographic profiles of recruits, their motivations, and the role of ideology and propaganda. It also takes into account the geopolitical framework conditions that promote the attractiveness of extremist ideologies.

Most European IS recruits are young men between the ages of 18 and 35. However, studies show that women and minors are also increasingly being recruited. Women make up about 10 to 15 percent of European IS supporters, often with the function of supporting the "Islamic State" as mothers of future fighters.

The educational backgrounds of IS recruits are heterogeneous. While some are well-educated and have a professional background in technology or medicine, many have low educational or professional qualifications. This discrepancy shows that there is no clear correlation between educational attainment and vulnerability to radicalisation.

A significant number of European IS fighters come from second- or third-generation migrant families, especially Muslim communities. Often these young people experience an identity crisis and feel neither fully integrated into their culture of origin nor into Western society. This "intermediate position" can make them more susceptible to radical ideologies that promise them a strong, clear identity.

The ideology of the "Islamic State" offers a worldview that is simple but powerful: a clear distinction between "good" and "evil" and the promise of an immediate reward in the afterlife for engagement in the "holy war". For many recruits, ISIS's ideology is attractive because it gives them a sense of belonging and purpose that they have lacked in their lives so far.

Radicalization rarely occurs in isolation, but often within social networks. Close friendships or family ties to people who have already been radicalized increase the likelihood that a person will become radicalized themselves. In some cases, entire families or groups of friends have traveled together to join ISIS.

The social and political marginalization of Muslims in Europe is often cited as one of the main factors for radicalization. Discrimination, economic disadvantage and the feeling of being excluded from society can drive young people into the arms of extremist groups that promise them power, respect and meaning.

ISIS has cleverly used social media and other online platforms to recruit young people. Professionally produced videos that depict heroic stories and the "paradise on earth" in the caliphate appeal especially to young, impressionable people. The virtual community built through social media can be just as strong as real-life communities, providing a platform for radical ideology to spread across national borders.

After recruitment, supporters often undergo intensive ideological training, which takes place online or in ISIS training camps. These trainings include both religious and military elements and aim to prepare recruits mentally and physically for jihad.

The conflicts in the Middle East, especially in Syria and Iraq, have created the breeding ground for the emergence and spread of IS. The destabilization of the region through external military intervention and internal power struggles has made it easier for extremists to recruit followers who want to fight against perceived injustices.

The foreign policies of European countries, especially their role in military interventions in the Middle East, have fueled resentment among certain Muslim communities in Europe. These policy decisions are often used by IS propagandists as evidence of Western "hostility" to Islam, facilitating recruitment efforts.

Preventing radicalisation requires a holistic approach that includes education, social inclusion and economic opportunities. Programs to promote social justice and combat discrimination are crucial to reducing vulnerability to radical ideologies.

Deradicalization programmes aim to reintegrate people who have already been radicalized into society. These programs include psychological care, social support and often religious rehabilitation measures to question and change the ideological beliefs of the people concerned.

The question of who becomes IS terrorists in Europe is complex and multi-layered. It encompasses a mixture of individual, social, political and ideological factors. While young people who are socially marginalized and in search of an identity seem to be particularly vulnerable, people from more stable backgrounds can also be radicalized. Tackling radicalisation therefore requires a comprehensive approach that includes both preventive and rehabilitative measures. The average age of IS Terrorists in Europe is 28.

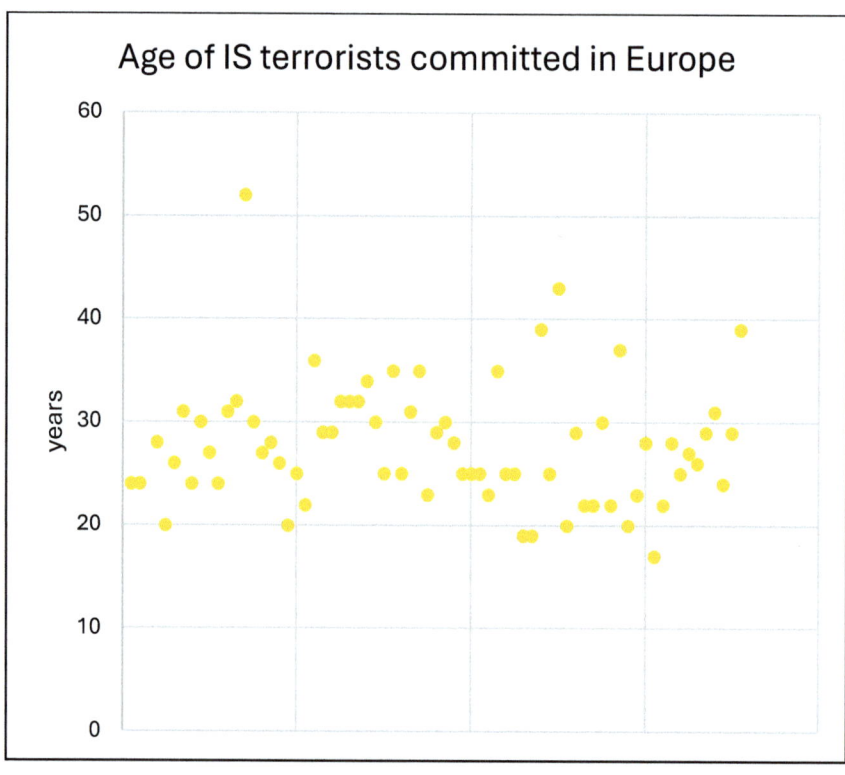

Studies on the death rate of IS terrorists in Europe show that about 63 percent of perpetrators are killed during their attacks. This high value can be attributed to various factors. A cen-

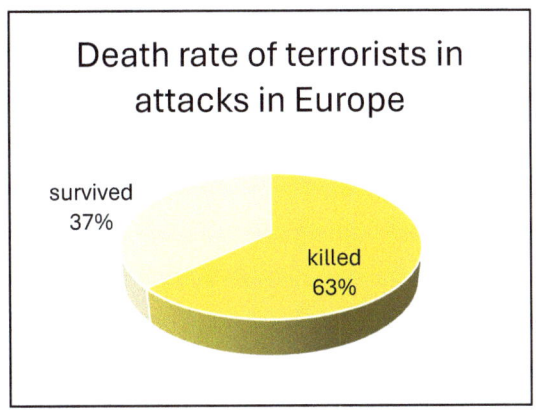

Death rate of terrorists in attacks in Europe

survived 37%

killed 63%

tral feature of the tactics of the "Islamic State" (IS) is the willingness of the perpetrators to accept death in the attacks, often in the context of suicide bombings or through confrontations with security forces. This approach is in line with ISIS's ideological orientation, which glorifies death in battle as martyrdom.

In addition, the rapid response capacity of European security agencies contributes to the fact that many attackers are killed during the attacks. Especially in urban areas with a high level of security, there is a high probability that terrorists will be stopped by targeted measures before they can cause further damage. This high mortality rate of IS terrorists illustrates the dangerous dynamics of modern terrorist attacks and the challenges for security agencies in Europe.

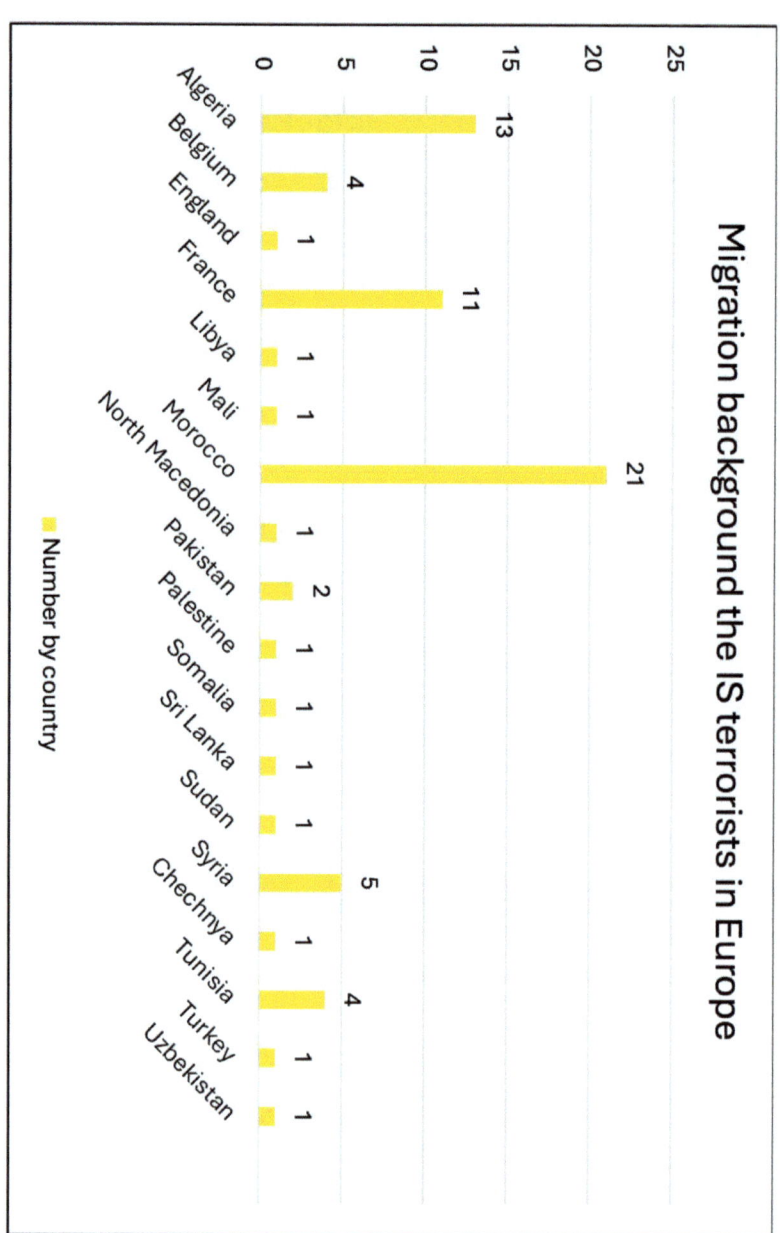

Migration background the IS terrorists in Europe

Country	Number by country
Algeria	13
Belgium	4
England	1
France	11
Libya	1
Mali	1
Morocco	21
North Macedonia	1
Pakistan	2
Palestine	1
Somalia	1
Sri Lanka	1
Sudan	1
Syria	5
Chechnya	1
Tunisia	4
Turkey	1
Uzbekistan	1

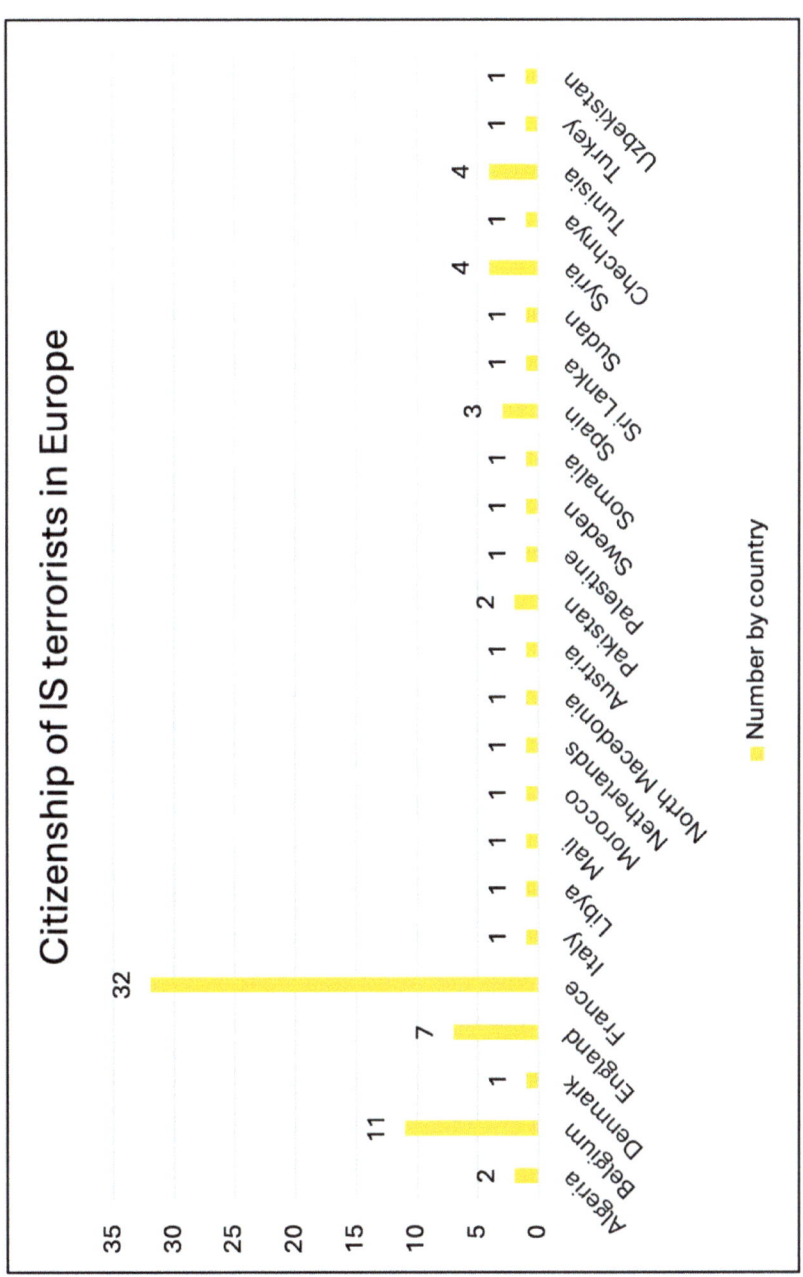

Citizenship of IS terrorists in Europe

■ Number by country

Country	Number
Algeria	2
Belgium	11
Denmark	1
England	7
France	32
Italy	1
Libya	1
Mali	1
Morocco	1
Netherlands	1
North Macedonia	1
Austria	1
Pakistan	2
Palestine	1
Sweden	1
Somalia	1
Spain	3
Sri Lanka	1
Sudan	1
Syria	4
Chechnya	1
Tunisia	4
Turkey	1
Uzbekistan	1

THREAT FROM IS IN THE PRESENT

Despite its territorial losses, the Islamic State (IS) remains a multifaceted and serious threat to global security. The group's adaptability is evident in its ability to change its tactics and strategies and adapt to new circumstances.

After losing its territorial strongholds in Syria and Iraq, IS has fundamentally changed its military strategies. Instead of conventional warfare, the organization is now increasingly relying on asymmetric warfare and guerrilla tactics. In the conflict-torn regions of Syria and Iraq, IS continues to carry out targeted attacks. These attacks are often directed against security forces, but also against civilians, especially against minority groups that are considered enemies of Islam in the eyes of IS.

ISIS can conduct complex and well-coordinated operations, ranging from ambushes on military convoys to suicide bombings in busy urban areas. These tactics are designed to undermine the population's trust in the state security forces and create the impression that ISIS remains a significant power. In addition, ISIS uses ungovernable or poorly controlled areas, especially in the rural regions of Syria and Iraq, as safe havens to reorganize, recruit new fighters and prepare attacks. Weak governance and persistent instability in these regions favor ISIS's ability to act as a kind of "shadow state" and maintain its presence.

The influence of IS is no longer limited to the Middle East. The organization has spread globally by building connections with regional groups and establishing offshoots in different parts of the world. These local ISIS cells, also known as "provinces," operate largely autonomously, but are ideologically and sometimes organizationally linked to ISIS's main core.

In Africa, ISIS has gained significant influence through its local branches, such as the Islamic State in the West African Province (ISWAP) and the Islamic State in the Greater Sahara (ISGS). These groups regularly carry out brutal attacks, often resulting in massive civilian casualties and contributing to the destabilization of entire regions. In the Sahel, a region already marked by ethnic tensions and state weakness, ISIS has filled a vacuum left by the failure of state institutions.

In Afghanistan, the Islamic State Khorasan Province (ISIS-K) has established itself as one of the most dangerous threats. Since the withdrawal of US troops and the Taliban's rise to power, ISIS-K has intensified its attacks, both against Taliban forces and against the civilian population, especially against religious and ethnic minorities such as the Hazara. These attacks are aimed at destabilizing the Taliban government and further polarizing the region.

In addition, IS is active in Southeast Asia, especially in the Philippines and Indonesia, as well as in Central Asia. In all these regions, IS pursues a strategy of local adaptation by exploiting existing conflicts and instrumentalizing local grievances to expand its influence.

The Islamic State has established itself as a leading ideological force in global jihadism. ISIS's ideological appeal remains strong despite its military defeats, particularly through its effective use of propaganda. ISIS propaganda is specifically designed to radicalize and inspire potential followers, whether by calling for hijra (emigrating to ISIS-controlled areas) or by promoting "lone wolves" attacks in their home countries.

ISIS's propaganda uses social media, encrypted communication channels and the dark web to spread its messages. It is often emotionally charged, using gruesome images and videos to incite fear while promoting a heroic narrative of ISIS's "martyrs." This content aims to mobilize anger and frustration and get potential fighters to join the global jihad or carry out terrorist attacks on their own. The challenge for security agencies is to monitor and stop this extremist content, which is an immense task given the decentralized nature of the Internet.

A particularly dangerous aspect of this radicalization strategy is the encouragement of "lone wolves" attacks. These attacks, in which individuals act without direct instructions or support from IS cells, are difficult to predict and prevent. Examples of this are attacks such as the one in Nice in 2016, in which a lone perpetrator drove a truck into a crowd of people and killed 86 people. Such attacks do not require complex logistics and can have devastating effects with minimal expenditure of resources.

Another complex threat comes from former IS fighters who return to their home countries or are released from captivity.

These returnees, often referred to as "foreign fighters", pose a significant security challenge, as many of them remain radicalized and may be planning violent attacks. In some cases, returnees have sought to build new networks or support existing cells by sharing their experience and skills gained in the Middle East.

Many of these fighters have become highly radicalized in the war zones and are particularly dangerous due to their combat experience and ideological convictions. The problem of returnees is exacerbated by the lack of comprehensive deradicalization programmes in many countries of origin. In some cases, there are also legal and political hurdles that make it difficult to prosecute these individuals, especially in the absence of evidence of their activities in ISIS areas.

In addition, the management and repatriation of family members, especially women and children, who have lived in IS areas pose another challenge. These individuals are often traumatized and ideologically influenced, which makes their integration into society difficult. The return of these family members can lead to social tensions in the countries of origin and increase the risk of the emergence of new extremist networks.

IS has also expanded its activities in the digital space, which represents a new dimension of threat. The group uses the internet not only to spread its ideology, but also to recruit, plan, and execute attacks. The digital infrastructure provides ISIS with a cost-effective and effective way to coordinate its global operations and mobilize its supporters.

A key aspect of this digital threat is the use of encrypted communication platforms that enable IS to evade surveillance by security agencies. Through these channels, ISIS coordinates operations, exchanges information and disseminates instructions to produce improvised explosive devices and other weapons. These instructions are often detailed and technically savvy, which allows even non-technical people to plan and carry out dangerous attacks.

In addition, ISIS has tried to carry out cyberattacks on critical infrastructure in Western countries. These attacks aim to cause significant disruption and undermine public trust in government institutions and the security of the digital world. While many of these attacks have so far failed or had limited success, the ongoing threat demonstrates the need for increased international cooperation in the field of cybersecurity.

THE ISLAMIC STATE AND THE FUTURE OF GLOBAL JIHADISM

Despite its territorial collapse in 2019, the Islamic State has left deep scars in the global security discourse. However, the decline of the caliphate and the deaths of leaders such as Abu Bakr al-Baghdadi and Abu Ibrahim al-Hashimi al-Qurashi have not completely wiped-out ISIS. Instead, ISIS has transformed into a more flexible and decentralized organization that is finding new ways to spread its ideology and violence.

The Islamic State after the Caliphate: A Decentralization of the Threat

After losing its territorial base, IS has resorted to a strategy of decentralization. This strategy is strongly reminiscent of the developments of other jihadist organizations such as al-Qaeda after September 11, 2001.

IS has transformed itself from a territorial organization into a globally active network that relies on flexible and loosely connected cells. While IS is militarily severely weakened in Iraq and Syria, it remains in a position to carry out attacks and guerrilla actions. Of particular note is ISIS's ability to establish regional offshoots, known as Wilayat, that operate in different parts of the world, including:

West Africa (ISWAP): ISIS remains active in Nigeria and the Sahel, taking advantage of weak state structures to carry out acts of terrorism and gain control over territories.

Afghanistan (IS-K): The Islamic State in Khorasan Province (IS-K) is one of the most dangerous offshoot groups that has been able to strengthen its power base after the withdrawal of US troops from Afghanistan in 2021.

Central Africa: In countries such as the Democratic Republic of Congo and Mozambique, IS has gained increasing influence by exploiting local conflicts and instability.

Decentralization makes it difficult to defeat ISIS once and for all, as the organization operates on several continents and adapts to different geopolitical realities. The ideological attachment to the vision of the caliphate remains, even if the physical realization of the caliphate seems to be out of reach now.

In its post-caliphate state, IS relies on a classic jihadist tactic: asymmetrical war. Instead of holding large territories, the group focuses on smaller attacks, guerrilla tactics, and terrorist attacks. This strategy can be seen in many parts of the world, especially in Syria and Iraq, where ISIS continues to carry out small but deadly attacks on security forces and civilians.

These tactics have also become visible in Europe and other Western countries, where the recruitment of lone wolves (so-called "lone wolves") plays a central role in ISIS's strategy. These lone perpetrators are often only loosely connected to the organization but motivated by their ideology. They use simple means, such as knife attacks or vehicular attacks, to spread fear and perpetuate the idea that ISIS is also active outside the Middle East.

The Future of Global Jihadism: New Threats and Challenges
In addition to IS, there are numerous jihadist movements that operate in a global context and benefit from the instability in certain regions. Al-Qaeda remains a central player in the jihadist spectrum and differs from IS in strategy and orientation.

A key factor for the future of global jihadism is the competition between ISIS and al-Qaeda. While both groups pursue similar ideological goals, namely the establishment of an Islamic state and the fight against the West, they differ in their methodology and tactics.

Al-Qaeda has become more focused on long-term goals since the death of Osama bin Laden, emphasizing the importance of gradually conquering territory and forming alliances with local groups. This strategy can be seen, for example, in al-Qaeda's cooperation with local militias in countries such as Yemen, Somalia and Mali.

ISIS, on the other hand, relies on a more radical and immediate approach, characterized by extreme brutality and spectacular acts of violence. ISIS is striving for immediate results, as was the case in the past with the proclamation of the caliphate. This has led to tensions between the two organizations, especially in regions where they are fighting for influence.

This rivalry could further fragment global jihadism and lead both groups to try to prove their relevance through spectacular attacks and military actions. It is conceivable that we will see an increase in attacks and regional conflicts in the coming years, as each organization fights for supremacy in jihadism.

Another important trend is the fragmentation of global jihadism. While organizations such as IS and al-Qaeda operate globally, more and more regional jihadist movements are emerging that use local conflicts and political instability for their own purposes. The Sahel region in Africa, Afghanistan, Yemen and the Middle East are particularly vulnerable to this form of regionalized jihadism.

This regionalization could make global jihadism even more difficult to control, as it is increasingly embedded in local conflicts. The danger is that regional actors will adopt and reinforce jihadist ideologies, which could lead to a perpetuation of violence and destabilization of entire regions.

Ideological and technological adaptability of ISIS and global jihadism

A key strength of ISIS and other jihadist groups is their ability to adapt their ideology to changing geopolitical and social conditions. Jihadist ideology is constantly evolving by responding to political, social and economic problems that arise especially in the Muslim world. IS and al-Qaeda use grievances such as corruption, economic inequality and the failure of the state to offer their ideology as a solution.

One example of this is the exploitation of the uncertainty after the Arab Spring. IS was able to gain a foothold in Syria and Iraq in particular, as the political systems in both countries had collapsed. This ability to respond to societal crises remains a crucial factor for the long-term survival of jihadist groups.

ISIS has proven that it is a master of technological adaptation. The use of social media and modern communication platforms for propaganda, recruitment and coordination of attacks is a central element of ISIS's strategy. Future technological innovations could create new threats:

Cyber terrorism: ISIS could expand its activities into cyberspace by planning cyberattacks on critical infrastructure in Western countries. So far, there are few concrete signs of this, but the possibility remains as jihadist groups increasingly acquire technical knowledge.

Drones and autonomous weapons: Another potential threat is the use of drones and autonomous weapon systems. ISIS has used drones for surveillance and attack missions in the past, and it is conceivable that this technology will be further developed in the future to cause greater damage.

The increasing availability and decreasing technical knowledge required to deploy such technologies could enable ISIS and other groups to carry out even more dangerous and unpredictable attacks.

The future of the Islamic State and global jihadism remains one of the greatest challenges to international security. While ISIS has been territorially defeated, its ideology remains alive, and its ability to adapt to new circumstances continues to make it dangerous. Global jihadism is becoming increasingly fragmented and regionalized, with competition between ISIS and al-Qaeda and the use of new technologies playing a central role.

The resilience of these movements, their ability to exploit local conflicts, and their technological adaptability make it difficult to completely eradicate global jihadism. The international community will continue to face a changing and dynamic threat in the coming years, which is constantly evolving and taking on new forms.

DERADICALIZATION: PREVENTION AND INTERVENTION

Deradicalization and prevention against radicalization by the Islamic State (IS) are central concerns in the fight against global terrorism. Given the threat posed by jihadist-Salafist groups such as ISIS, strategies to prevent radicalisation and reintegrate radicalized individuals into society are crucial. These strategies include a wide range of measures, ranging from preventive approaches to targeted interventions. In this context, deradicalization programmes play a crucial role.

Radicalization is a process in which individuals or groups adopt extreme political, religious, or ideological views that can lead them to engage in violent behavior. In the case of ISIS, radicalization often leads to support or participation in terrorist activities aimed at establishing a caliphate through violence and terror.

Initial receptivity: Individuals become receptive to extremist ideologies due to personal, political, or social dissatisfaction. **Indoctrination:** In this phase, they adopt the extremist ideologies and begin to see them as the solution to their problems. **Mobilization:** This eventually leads to active support or participation in extremist or terrorist activities.

Prevention aims to nip the radicalisation process in the bud before it leads to violent extremism. Preventive measures are usually broad-based and target vulnerable communities, especially young people. These include:

Education and awareness: Education is a key tool for preventing radicalisation. Programs that promote critical thinking, intercultural competence, and knowledge of religious and political issues can help protect youth from extremist ideologies. Awareness campaigns that provide information about the dangers of extremism and the methods of recruitment by terrorist organizations are also important.

Strengthening social inclusion: Many people become radicalized due to social isolation, discrimination or the feeling of not belonging to society. Promoting social inclusion through community programs, job-search assistance, and psychological support can help address these root causes.

Online prevention: With ISIS and other terrorist organizations making extensive use of the internet and social media to spread their ideologies and recruit new members, online prevention is crucial. Initiatives to monitor and counter extremist content online, as well as the promotion of alternative narratives, are essential components of this strategy.

Deradicalization: Intervention in Radicalized Individuals Deradicalization programmes target people who have already been radicalized or are in the early stages of radicalisation. These programmes aim to deconstruct the extremist beliefs of those affected and to show them ways to peaceful and productive reintegration into society.

Psychological and religious counselling: Many deradicaliza-tion programmes rely on the combination of psychological support and religious education. Psychologists work to treat deep-rooted beliefs and trauma, while religious counselors help correct the misinterpretations of religious texts that led to radicalization.

Education and work programmes: Reintegration into society often requires practical support. Educational programmes that provide new skills to those affected and programmes to help them find a job are important elements of deradicaliza-tion. These programs aim to provide positive prospects for the future.

Family and community support: Involving families and com-munities in the deradicalization process is crucial. Family members can play an important role by providing emotional support and helping those affected break away from extremist networks. Community programmes aimed at the reintegration of those affected can also help to prevent relapses into ex-tremist behavior.

Despite the importance of deradicalization and prevention programmes, there are numerous challenges. One of the big-gest challenges is that radicalisation is a complex and individ-ually varying process. There is no universal solution that works equally for all radicalized individuals or communities. In addi-tion, it is often difficult to measure the success of deradicalization programs, as relapses into extremist behavior are not always immediately obvious.

Another problem is the scarcity of resources. Many countries do not have sufficient resources to implement comprehensive prevention and deradicalization programmes. This is especially the case in countries already affected by conflict and instability, and where radical groups such as ISIS operate.

There are some countries that have developed successful deradicalization programs. One example is the Saudi Arabian Deradicalization Program, which has been active since 2004. It combines religious counseling, psychological care, education, and social support. The program has managed to rehabilitate a significant number of former extremists and reintegrate them into society.

Another example is the Indonesian deradicalization program, which focuses on the reintegration of former terrorists. It includes religious re-education, economic support, and the use of former terrorists as spokesmen to fight extremism.

In view of the continuing threat from IS and other extremist groups, the further development and adaptation of prevention and deradicalization strategies remains an urgent necessity. In particular, the development of tailor-made programmes that consider local cultural and social conditions, as well as increased international cooperation, are crucial to meet these challenges.

In addition, the role of technology in prevention and deradicalization will become increasingly important. In the future, artificial intelligence and big data could help to identify people at risk at an early stage and enable targeted interventions.

Deradicalization and prevention against radicalisation by IS are complex and multi-faceted tasks that require a comprehensive approach. Preventive measures must target the root causes of radicalisation, while deradicalization programmes must be individually adapted to be successful in the long term. Despite the challenges associated with these efforts, they offer one of the best opportunities to curb the spread of violent extremism and shape a more peaceful future.

MEDIA COVERAGE OF TERRORIST ATTACKS

Terrorist attacks are cruel events that not only cause great suffering, but also have a profound social impact. In addition to the immediate physical damage and psychological trauma they cause, they also pose a challenge to the media that must report on these incidents. In today's globally interconnected world, terrorists often rely on media coverage to spread their messages and achieve their goals. Therefore, the way media report on terrorist attacks and their perpetrators is crucial.

A central point of discussion in media ethics and terrorism research is the question of whether and to what extent reporting on terrorists can potentially motivate others to commit similar acts. Particularly controversial is the publication of pictures, names and biographical information of the perpetrators. The hypothesis that this could encourage imitation has gained weight in recent years through scientific studies.

Terrorism is a communication strategy. Terrorists rely on violence to spread fear, and media coverage acts as a multiplier. Terrorism researcher Alex Schmid describes this as "propaganda by the deed". Terrorist attacks aim to attract attention, and this attention is significantly amplified by the media. The media play the role of a catalyst by informing the audience about the event and interpreting it. According to Schmid, terrorism cannot have the same impact without media coverage, as the attack itself targets a comparatively small group, while reporting makes the event accessible to a global audience.

A 2014 study by Paul Gill and John Horgan shows that media content has played a role in the radicalisation and mobilization of individuals in many cases. Especially in the case of "lone wolves" – lone perpetrators who act without direct support from an organization – media reports about previous attacks can serve as inspiration. Terrorists such as Anders Breivik, the mass murderer of Utøya, and the Christchurch attacker in 2019 have explicitly cited previous terrorist attacks as a source of inspiration in their manifestos and public statements. Such perpetrators often strive to surpass their "role models" and to stage their deeds even more effectively in the media.

The so-called "copycat effect" describes the phenomenon that the disclosure of a crime inspires other potential perpetrators to commit similar acts. In recent years, numerous studies have provided evidence that this effect also plays a role in terrorist attacks. A comprehensive analysis of mass shootings and terrorist attacks by researchers Sherry Towers and Andres Gomez-Lievano found that after a major attack, the likelihood of another similar attack is significantly increased for a certain period. It was particularly striking that media coverage played a catalytic role in this.

The researchers looked at data from mass shootings in the U.S. between 2006 and 2011 and found that one incident within 13 days was followed by another when media coverage was particularly intense. This "clustering" of violent crimes shows that perpetrators could be motivated by the public presentation of such acts. Similar patterns can also be observed in terrorist attacks, especially when the perpetrators explicitly seek attention, as is often the case with Islamist and right-wing extremist perpetrators.

The media focus on perpetrators – especially through the dissemination of photos, videos and biographical details – has a demonstrable impact on the perception of the perpetrators and the potential for imitation. Psychologist Jennifer Johnston of Western New Mexico University has developed a theory known as the "Media Contagion Theory." It argues that extensive reporting on perpetrators that operates with images and names can lead to the "glorification" of these perpetrators. Potential copycat perpetrators see that a terrorist attack or rampage can generate immense media attention. This can serve as an incentive to commit similar acts themselves to be present in public discourse as well.

This is particularly problematic for loners or ideologically motivated perpetrators who already have a need for recognition and attention. The Christchurch attacker in 2019 streamed his act live on the internet and used social media to spread his ideology. Through the subsequent worldwide reporting, his act was replicated and amplified millions of times. In such cases, reporting can help the perpetrators achieve their goals, which in turn could inspire others to commit similar acts.

In view of the potential impact of reporting on terrorist attacks, the question arises as to how the media can act in an ethically responsible manner. The challenge is to find a balance between the public need for information and the avoidance of possible glorification of perpetrators. Experts and media ethicists have developed several guidelines that could serve as guides:

Reduction of the focus on perpetrators: Many experts advocate diverting attention away from the perpetrators and instead focusing on the victims' stories. Such an approach could help to ensure that perpetrators are not perceived as "stars" of reporting, but as criminals whose actions must be condemned. This could also help minimize the psychological impact on victims' relatives, who often feel that too much attention is being paid to the perpetrators.

Refrain from publishing pictures of perpetrators: One of the most effective measures to reduce the potential for imitation could be to refrain from publishing pictures and names of the perpetrators. A 2018 study by Adam Lankford and Eric Madfis suggests that perpetrators who do not gain visual and name recognition are less likely to be impersonated. This could be especially significant in the case of "lone wolves", who often aspire to some kind of celebrity.

Limiting detailed information about the crime: Publishing detailed descriptions of the crimes and the tactics of the perpetrators should be avoided. This could serve as a "guide" for potential copycats. More restrained reporting, which is limited to the essentials and dispenses with sensational details, could reduce the risk of imitation.

Emphasis on prevention and resilience: Instead of just reporting on the attack itself, the media should also report on measures to prevent and rebuild after such events. This can reduce the feeling of powerlessness and fear in society and strengthen resilience. Focusing on positive aspects of recovery and cohesion after a terrorist attack could help to regain narrative control and move the perpetrators out of focus.

Legal framework and voluntary media guidelines

Some countries have responded to the problem of the portrayal of perpetrators by introducing legal measures or voluntary guidelines for the media. After the terrorist attacks of 2015, France took certain measures to prevent the spread of extremist content and make it more difficult to access radical ideologies. There are also initiatives in Germany and the USA that deal with ethical reporting on terrorism.

In Canada, after an attack in 2018, police went so far as to deliberately withhold the name of the perpetrator so as not to provide a stage for his ideology. Similarly, some media companies have developed voluntary guidelines that regulate the handling of images and names of perpetrators. The German Press Council, for example, has formulated guidelines that encourage journalists to carefully consider the naming of perpetrators and to give preference to the victims.

Media coverage of terrorist attacks faces a difficult challenge. On the one hand, there is a legitimate public interest in information about such events, but on the other hand, the type of reporting carries the risk of unintentionally offering terrorists a platform. Research clearly shows that intensive reporting on perpetrators has the potential to inspire others to commit similar acts. This is especially true if images of perpetrators and biographical details are prominently disseminated.

One solution could be to reduce the focus on perpetrators and instead focus on victims' stories, prevention measures and societal resilience. The media must live up to their responsibility to inform the public without contributing to the glorification of violence and terrorism. Voluntary guidelines and legal measures can help to ensure a responsible approach to this sensitive issue and minimize the risk of copycat offenders.

DEALING WITH RETURNEES: CHALLENGES FOR WESTERN STATES

Dealing with returnees from the Islamic State poses considerable legal, security and social challenges for Western states. These individuals, who traveled to conflict zones to join a terrorist organization, are now returning to their home countries or seeking to return. The complexity of the problem results from a variety of factors: the legal classification of returnees, security concerns, deradicalization measures and societal implications.

Those who have traveled to Syria and Iraq to join ISIS in recent years have come from various Western countries and represent a wide range of demographics. They are men and women of different age groups, socio-economic backgrounds and educational levels. Many of these individuals were already radicalized before their departure, while others were seduced by ISIS propaganda and recruitment tactics. The returnees include both fighters and non-combatants such as spouses and children.

The roles played by returnees in the IS caliphate vary greatly. While some were directly involved in violent crimes as combatants, others worked in administrative, logistical or propaganda positions. Women who joined ISIS were often forced to adopt traditional gender roles, with many being forced into marriage or giving birth to children under adverse conditions.

220

The experiences of returnees in the conflict areas are marked by violence, trauma and, in many cases, disillusionment with ISIS's ideology.

The criminal prosecution of IS returnees poses considerable legal challenges for Western countries. Proving that a person has joined ISIS or has been involved in crimes requires extensive evidence, which is often difficult to obtain. In many cases, there is a lack of concrete evidence, as the acts were committed in a war zone without constitutional structures. Videos, photos or testimonies can be difficult to verify or insufficient to stand up in a court.

Some Western countries have tried to prevent returnees from returning to their home country by revoking their citizenship. However, this is legally controversial, especially with regard to international law, which prohibits states from making people stateless. Citizenship revocation is often seen as a last resort and is met with criticism both nationally and internationally, as it calls into question the state's responsibility to its citizens and creates legal uncertainty.

There are legal challenges in dealing with the children of IS fighters who were born in the conflict areas or brought there. These children are often stateless and bear the burden of their parents' actions. Their return and integration into Western societies raise questions of child welfare, citizenship and possible radicalisation. At the same time, there is an ethical obligation to protect these children and enable them to live in safety and dignity.

A central security policy concern is the risk that returnees could pose a threat to internal security. Some returnees may continue to be radicalized and potentially plan or carry out terrorist attacks in their home countries. In addition, there is a risk that returnees in prisons or within their communities will act as recruiters for extremist networks, thus spreading radicalisation.

The surveillance of returnees requires considerable resources from security authorities and intelligence services. In many Western countries, the surveillance of potentially dangerous individuals is an essential part of the national security strategy. However, even with intensive surveillance, there remains a risk that some returnees could plan or carry out terrorist activities unnoticed. The balance between security and the rights of those affected poses constant challenges for the authorities.

Effective deradicalization and reintegration of returnees is crucial to minimize the risk of re-radicalisation. Western countries have developed different approaches to reintegrate returnees into society, with a focus on psychological care, social support and the teaching of alternative ideologies. However, these programs often face the challenge of being sufficiently effective, and it remains unclear how successful they will be in the long term. There are also debates about how best to allocate resources to deradicalization programmes and which target groups are most in need of support.

Dealing with returnees is a sensitive topic that is often controversially discussed in public. Many citizens have reservations or fears about the return of people who have joined IS. This skepticism makes it difficult for returnees to reintegrate, as social prejudices and stigmatization can hinder their return to a normal life. The media play an important role in shaping opinion and can spread both positive and negative narratives about returnees.

Many returnees, especially women and children, suffer from considerable psychological trauma due to their experiences in the conflict areas. Providing adequate psychological care and support is crucial to help these people process their experiences and lead a stable life. At the same time, the affected communities and social services are often not sufficiently prepared for the special needs of this group, which can lead to gaps in care.

The successful integration of returnees into educational institutions and the labour market is a decisive factor for their long-term resocialization. However, this poses a significant challenge, as many returnees struggle to find work or training due to their experiences in IS and the stigma associated with it. Education and labour market programmes that are specifically tailored to the needs of returnees can help overcome these hurdles.

Overcoming the challenges of dealing with IS returnees requires close international cooperation. The exchange of information between the security services of different states is crucial to monitor the movements of returnees and to identify possible threats at an early stage. At the same time, Western states need to develop joint strategies to ensure coordinated action and maximize the effectiveness of prevention and deradicalization programs.

Cooperation with the countries of origin and transit of IS fighters is also of central importance. Many returnees originally come from countries in the Middle East or North Africa or have passed through these countries on their way to the conflict zones. Effective repatriation and integration require cooperation with these states to ensure that returnees do not reach their home countries unnoticed and pose a threat there again.

In the long term, preventing radicalisation and promoting deradicalization in a global context is essential to prevent the return of extremist fighters. This requires both local initiatives in the affected countries and global efforts to address the underlying causes of radicalisation – such as poverty, marginalization and ideological indoctrination. Education, social integration and the promotion of tolerance and intercultural dialogue play a key role in this.

Dealing with returnees from IS presents Western countries with a multitude of complex challenges that include legal, security and social aspects. While the threat of radicalized returnees is real, states must also carefully consider the legal and ethical implications of their actions. Deradicalization and reintegration of these individuals is crucial to ensure long-term security while upholding the principles of the rule of law and human rights. International cooperation and a comprehensive approach that includes both preventive and reactive measures are essential to effectively address these challenges and find a sustainable solution to the problem of IS returnees.

LESSONS FROM THE RISE AND FALL OF IS FOR FUTURE COUNTER-TERRORISM STRATEGIES

The Islamic State has played a key role in recent history as one of the most dangerous and influential terrorist organizations on a global scale. Through its brutal methods, effective propaganda and ability to mobilize supporters worldwide, ISIS posed not only a military but also an ideological challenge. Understanding the mechanisms that have made IS so dangerous is crucial to developing future counterterrorism strategies that can effectively prevent Islamist attacks.

Ideological radicalisation and preventive measures
Ideological radicalization is a central element of ISIS, which has enabled it to gain followers across geographical borders. ISIS's propaganda aimed to radicalize young people by

presenting a distorted image of Islam and world politics that justifies violence and terrorism as legitimate means of achieving political and religious goals.

Radicalisation does not happen overnight, but is a gradual process influenced by various factors. These include personal crises, identity problems, the search for belonging and exposure to extremist ideology. IS used social media and other online platforms to target these people. Propaganda videos idealizing the caliphate and glorifying brutal violence were circulated to recruit sympathizers.

Governments and international organizations must work closely together to identify and remove extremist content online. This requires not only technical monitoring, but also working with social media companies to develop algorithms that efficiently detect radical content.

It is not enough to delete radical content; it is also necessary to create positive counter-narratives that refute the extremist messages of IS. These counter-narratives should be disseminated by credible actors, such as moderate Muslim scholars, activists, and community leaders.

Schools and communities play a crucial role in preventing radicalisation. Educational programs should aim to educate young people about the dangers of extremist ideologies and promote critical thinking. It is important that these programs are designed to be culturally sensitive and respect the complexity of finding identity.

People who show signs of radicalisation should be supported by social services and psychological support at an early stage. Cooperation between social services, schools and security authorities is crucial to identify people at risk and intervene in good time.

ISIS was characterized by a complex and flexible organizational structure that gave it an astonishing resilience despite military setbacks. This structure is decentralized and operates at various levels, from central command commands to autonomous cells and supporters worldwide.

Decentralization allowed ISIS to remain active even after losing territory. Individual cells operated autonomously, which made it difficult to dismantle the entire organization. These networks are often divided into different areas such as finance, recruitment, and propaganda, which operated independently of each other but are coordinated with each other.

The targeted identification and elimination of IS leaders can significantly weaken the coordination and coherence of the group. This requires sophisticated intelligence operations that focus on collecting communications data, movement patterns, and financial transactions.

ISIS's ability to operate depended largely on its communication. The targeted disruption and paralysis of these communication channels, for example through cyber operations, is an effective method of restricting the group's ability to act.

ISIS financed itself through a variety of sources, including illegal oil sales, human trafficking, extortion and donations. To weaken the financial basis of such organizations, international cooperation is needed that focuses on tracking and stopping these illicit money flows. This includes measures such as sanctioning financial institutions suspected of supporting terrorist financing, as well as monitoring donation flows.

Cooperation with local security forces and militias in the affected areas is essential to gather information and provide operational support. Local forces often have a better understanding of the conditions on the ground and can be more effective in identifying IS cells.

ISIS exploited the weaknesses of conventional armies by resorting to unconventional methods, such as suicide bombings, improvised explosive devices (IEDs) and the use of civilian shields. To combat future terrorist groups using similar tactics more effectively, conventional military strategies must be adapted and further developed.

One of the most important lessons from the fight against IS is the need to closely interlink intelligence operations with military operations. This makes it possible to better understand the enemy's movements and take preventive measures.

Military units must be specially prepared for the unconventional tactics of terrorist groups. This requires specialized training in urban warfare, the use of IEDs, and the development of techniques to minimize collateral damage. In addition, military units should be equipped with state-of-the-art technology to detect and neutralize booby traps and hidden attackers.

Strengthening cooperation with local militias: IS often operated in areas where local militias acted either as adversaries or potential allies. Cooperation with these militias can be crucial in gaining information and ensuring acceptance among the population. However, this collaboration requires careful management to ensure that local forces are not motivated by their own agendas or resentments.

Psychological warfare and propaganda
ISIS has been a master at using psychological warfare and propaganda to spread fear and terror. The dissemination of violent videos, the staging of atrocities and targeted disinformation have been used to undermine the morale of opponents and inspire potential followers.

Combating ISIS's psychological warfare
The psychological dimension of the war against IS must is not underestimated. Terrorism aims to achieve political goals by

spreading fear. Combating these tactics requires both offensive and defensive measures.

Counter-statements and information campaigns: The dissemination of counterstatements to terrorist propaganda actions is crucial to reduce their impact. These campaigns were aimed at exposing the reality of the ideology propagated by terrorists and showing the cruelty of their actions. In addition, information campaigns should strengthen the resilience of the population by pointing out that the purpose of terrorist acts is to spread fear and divide society.

Protecting civilians from psychological warfare: Civilians are often the primary target of terrorist attacks, as they aim to create maximum panic. Measures to protect the population should therefore not only be of a physical nature, but also include psychological support. These include programs that treat post-attack trauma and promote resilience to terrorism. This can be done through psychological care, education and support in coping with anxiety and stress.

Global cooperation in media surveillance: Terrorist groups such as IS use the Internet to spread their propaganda worldwide. Therefore, global cooperation is needed to curb the spread of this content. This can be achieved through joint initiatives to monitor and remove extremist content, as well as cooperation between governments and technology companies.

International cooperation and legal framework

The global threat posed by ISIS has highlighted the need for international cooperation in the fight against terrorism. No country can successfully tackle such a complex and interconnected threat on its own. The creation of a coherent international framework for counterterrorism is therefore essential.

Promotion of international cooperation

An effective counter-terrorism strategy requires close cooperation between states and the harmonization of the legal framework.

Common information and data exchange platforms: The establishment of common platforms for the exchange of intelligence information and data on known or suspected terrorists can help to close security gaps and combat cross-border threats more efficiently. These include agreements on the extradition of terror suspects and the sharing of surveillance data.

Harmonization of anti-terrorism legislation: Different legal frameworks can make it easier for terrorists to hide in certain countries or coordinate their activities. The creation of a single legal framework that allows for the cross-border prosecution and detention of terrorists is therefore crucial. This includes adapting asylum and immigration laws to prevent extremists from entering the country.

Coordinated military and police operations: Multinational operations under a common command and with coordinated strategies are often more effective than isolated national operations. The creation of multinational task forces that conduct joint operations can significantly increase the effectiveness of counterterrorism.

Strengthening international justice: Prosecuting war crimes and terrorist activities at the international level is crucial to ensure that perpetrators are held accountable. The International Criminal Court (ICC) plays an important role in prosecuting terrorists involved in atrocities. The support and strengthening of such institutions are therefore necessary to preserve the international legal order.

ISIS is a succinct example of the challenges that modern terrorist organizations pose to global security. The comprehensive analysis of its structures, methods and the reaction of the international community shows that a successful counter-terrorism strategy must consider not only military, but also political, economic, ideological and social aspects. Preventive measures against radicalisation, the dismantling of decentralized networks, the adaptation of military tactics and the strengthening of international cooperation are crucial to minimize the threat of Islamist attacks in the future. A coordinated and comprehensive approach that integrates all these elements can form the basis for sustainable success in the fight against terrorism. By taking into account the lessons learned from the fight against ISIS, future counterterrorism missions can be better prepared to meet the complex challenges of modern terrorist threats.

LITERATURE

Hassan Abu Hanieh: *IS und Al-Qaida. The crisis of the Sunnis and the rivalry in the global jihad.* German by Günther Orth. Dietz, Bonn 2016, ISBN 978-3-8012-0483-9.

Wilfried Buchta: *Terror vor Europas Toren. The Islamic State, Iraq's disintegration and America's powerlessness.* Campus Verlag, Frankfurt am Main, 2015, ISBN 978-3-593-50290-8.

Patrick Cockburn: *The Rise of Islamic State: ISIS and the New Sunni Revolution.* Verso, London/Brooklyn 2015, ISBN 978-1-78478-040-1.

Fawaz A. Gerges: *Isis. A History.* Princeton University Press, Princeton, New Jersey, USA 2016, ISBN 978-0-691-17000-8.

Christoph Günther: *A second state in Mesopotamia? Genesis and Ideology of the "Islamic State of Iraq".* Ergon, Würzburg 2014, ISBN 978-3-95650-036-7 (in the series *Culture, Law and Politics in Muslim Societies.* Volume 28, also dissertation at the University of Leipzig 2013)

Rainer Hermann: *Endstation Islamic State? State Failure and Religious War in the Arab World.* Deutscher Taschenbuch Verlag, Munich 2015, ISBN 978-3-423-34861-4.

Tristan Leoni: Caliphate and Barbarism – How Does the Islamic State Work? Translated from the French by Doc Sportello. bahoe books, Vienna 2016, ISBN 978-3-903022-37-9.

William McCants: *The ISIS Apocalypse: The History, Strategy, and Doomsday Vision of the Islamic State*. St. Martin's Press, New York 2016, ISBN 978-1-250-11264-4.

Hamideh Mohagheghi (Hrsg.): *Frauen für den Djihad*. The manifesto of the IS fighters; in Arabic and German. Herder, Freiburg 2015, ISBN 978-3-451-34832-7.

Loretta Napoleoni: *The Return of the Caliphate. The Islamic State and the Reorganization of the Middle East*. Translated from the English by Peter Stäuber. Rotpunktverlag, Zurich 2015, ISBN 978-3-85869-640-3. (Original: *The Islamist Phoenix. The Islamic State and the Redrawing of the Middle East*. 2014)

Petra Ramsauer: *The Jihad Generation. How the apocalyptic cult of the Islamic State threatens Europe*. Styria Verlag, Vienna 2015, ISBN 978-3-222-13516-3.

Christoph Reuter: *Die schwarze Macht. The "Islamic State" and the strategists of terror*. Deutsche Verlags-Anstalt, Munich 2015, ISBN 978-3-421-04694-9.

Christoph Reuter and Maryam A.: *My Life in the Caliphate. A German IS dropout tells her story*. Deutsche Verlags-Anstalt, Munich 2017, ISBN 978-3-421-04819-6.

Behnam T. Said: *Islamic State. IS-Miliz, al-Qaida und die deutschen Brigaden*. C.H. Beck, Munich 2014, ISBN 978-3-406-67210-1. (also known as the licensed edition of the BPB published, Volume 1546, Bonn 2015)

Bruno Schirra: *ISIS – The Global Jihad. How the "Islamic State" brings terror to Europe.* Econ, Berlin 2015, ISBN 978-3-430-20193-3.

Thomas Schmidinger: *"The World Has Forgotten Us". The genocide of the "Islamic State" against the Yazidis and the consequences.* Mandelbaum Verlag, Vienna 2019, ISBN 978-3-85476-590-5.

Thomas Carl Schwoerer: *Negotiating with IS? New solutions for Syria and terrorism.* Redline Verlag, Munich 2016, ISBN 978-3-86881-652-5.

Guido Steinberg: *Caliphate of Terror. IS and the threat of Islamist terror.* Knaur, Munich 2015, ISBN 978-3-426-78772-4.

Jessica Stern, J. M. Berger: *ISIS: The State of Terror.* HarperCollins, New York City 2015, ISBN 978-0-06-239554-2.

Jürgen Todenhöfer: *Inside IS – 10 Days in the 'Islamic State'.* 17th edition. C. Bertelsmann, Munich 2015, ISBN 978-3-570-10276-3.

Joby Warrick: *Black Flags. The rise of IS and the USA.* German by Cornelius Hartz. Theiss, Darmstadt 2017, ISBN 978-3-8062-3477-0.

Michael Weiss, Hassan Hassan: *ISIS: Inside the Army of Terror.* Regan Arts, New York 2015, ISBN 978-1-941393-57-4.